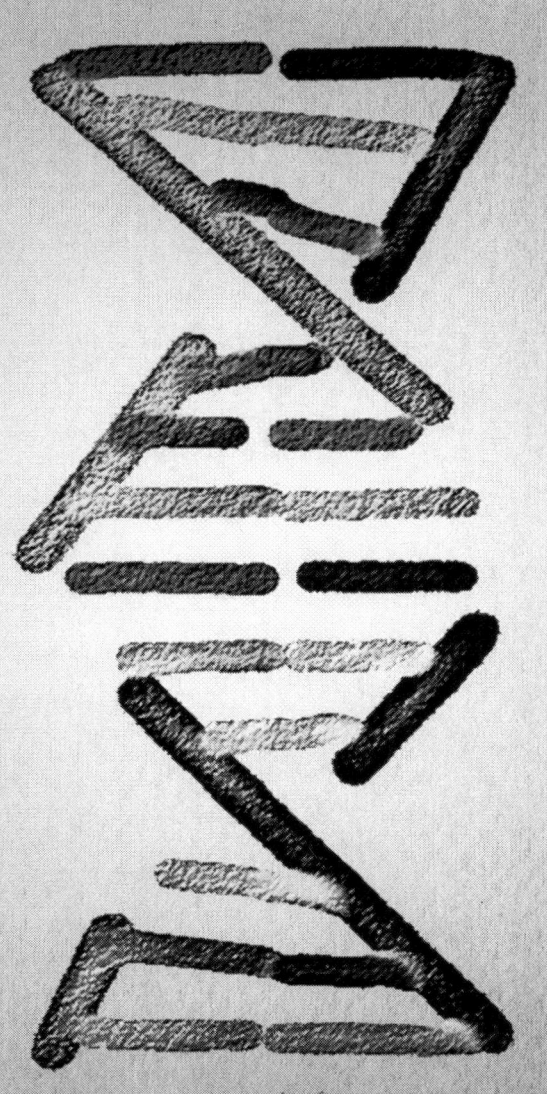

Ezekiel

AN ANTHOLOGY
OF EXPRESSIVE WORKS
BY PEOPLE LIVING WITH ALS
AND THEIR CAREGIVERS

VOICES FOR THE CURE

EDITED BY ERIC VALOR
WITH PAUL ROWE

CAUSEWAY BOOKS

Voices for the Cure: An Anthology of Expressive Works by People Living with ALS and Their Caregivers / Eric Valor, editor; with Paul Rowe. 1. Body, Mind & Spirit —Inspiration & Personal Growth. 2. Biography & Autobiography — People with Disabilities. 3. Literary Collections —Essays.

First Printing, 2022
Printed in the United States of America

Causeway Books, an imprint of Pen & Anvil Press
37 Boulder Drive
Fitchburg, Mass. 01420
www.penandanvil.com/causeway

Bulk discounts are available on quantity orders.
For trade and wholesale orders, or orders to corporations, associations, and others, contact the publisher at the address above.

Contents

- - - - - - - - - - - - - -

ONLINE AT WWW.PENANDANVIL.COM/VOICES

Small Eternities

TO EXPERIENCE ALS IN ANY CAPACITY IS HORRIFYING. THE most horrifying part being that it robs us of the most precious gift we get as humans: time. ALS shatters any illusions of control. It decimates our number of days. It ends a chapter we were in the middle of writing and never asks for our opinion on the matter.

While ALS seems all-consuming, reaching its scraggly fingers into each corner of our lives, there is one thing that ALS can never touch—the choice of how one is going to live with the time that is left. It's easy to make this claim as one who has never had ALS, so here is where I must introduce you to my Dad, David Brattain, who lived with ALS from 2015-2019. I saw with my own eyes as he made the choice to refuse to let a looming expiration date determine how each day might go. Through love, gratitude, perspective, and faith he took the three and a half years we had after diagnosis and packed them with joy and life.

It would be wrong to paint a rainbow over Dad's experience with ALS. His choice to live positively and with hope was beautiful because it was done so in the face of immense pain, heartache, shock, confusion and disappointment. Dad's three and a half years with ALS were marked by swollen fingers, episodes of choking, working together to lift him out of bed, putting on and tying his shoes, spoon feeding him each meal, watching him grimace as he tried to swallow his pills, and many more experiences that never should have become normal for my family.

And yet, amidst all of this, I saw my Dad shine. Each day he woke up and made the choice to have courage, to persevere, to be present with others, to serve, and to relish his favorite pleasures of this life. To him, that was the only choice to make.

Dad showed me that ALS may determine the quantity of our days, but it does not have to determine the quality of them. This disease forced us to acknowledge that all of our days on earth are slipping away, leaving behind a choice of how we will respond.

So, from my experience, here are some ways to respond. Hold the swollen fingers. Close your eyes and memorize the sound of their voice. Hug them whenever you feel the urge. Say what you want to say, even if it seems silly or bold. Savor each day and moment for the small yet incredible morsels of life that they are.

ALS took a lot from my family. But one thing it gave us was the grace of realizing time was slipping out of our hands—and if we wanted to, we could take the remaining years, months, weeks, or days and make them our own small eternities.

EMMA WOLFE

GLOSSARY

To aid readers, the editors wish to provide starting-point definitions of some key terms, abbreviations and concepts they will encounter in this anthology:

ALS or Amyotrophic Lateral Sclerosis - From www.als.net/als-resources/glossary: "Also known as Lou Gehrig's disease, ALS is a progressive neurodegenerative disease that affects the motor neurons in the brain (upper motor neurons) and spinal cord (lower motor neurons) which control the movement of muscles. The disorder causes muscle weakness, atrophy, and ultimately paralysis. Other symptoms could include fatigue, thick or slurred speech, and difficulty breathing and/or swallowing . . . There is no known cure."

ALS TDI - The ALS Therapy Development Institute is a non-profit biotechnology research organization based in Cambridge, Massachusetts, whose research teams focus on the search for effective treatments for ALS.

CALS - Caregivers of persons with ALS

CPAP - Continuous positive airway pressure is a form of non-invasive ventilation in which a constant level of pressure is continuously applied to the upper respiratory tract of a person. The application of positive pressure may be intended to prevent upper airway collapse.

CRISPR - This acronym, standing for clustered regularly interspaced short palindromic repeats, is a new genetic technology that uses segments of bacterial DNA to target and edit genes with great precision.

DynaVox - This Swedish company manufactures and distributes speech-generating, symbol-adapted, and communication software and hardware to assist individuals in overcoming speech, language and learning challenges.

EAP - Expanded access policies, also known as compassionate use, involves the use of an early-stage or unapproved drug or medical therapies by people with serious or life-threatening conditions who do not meet the enrollment criteria for clinical research trials

Eighteen Months - This length of time is often cited as the average life expectancy for a person diagnosed with ALS.

EMG - Electromyography is a medical procedure to assess the health of muscles and the motor neurons or nerve cells that control them. Since ALS affects the motor neurons, EMG is an important diagnostic tool for evaluating the condition of persons with ALS.

Hoyer Lift - Also known as patient lifts when not manufactured by the Hoyer corporation, lifts are assistive devices that allow patients with limited mobility to be transferred between a bed and a chair or similar resting places. They may be powered (electric) or unpowered.

MND or Motor Neuron Disease - MND is a dysfunction of the nerves which control the muscles, marked by progressive weakness and eventually death due to respiratory failure or aspiration. ALS is a variety of MND with the characteristic feature of gradual onset of weakness on one limb, which spreads to the other limbs and trunk muscles.

NurOwn - An investigational therapy under development by Brain-Storm Cell Therapeutics intended to slow the progression of ALS symptoms, involving the use of autologous mesenchymal stem cells (MSCs) and neurotrophic factors (NTFs).

PALS - Persons with ALS

RTT - Right-to-try laws were created with the intent of allowing terminally ill patients access to experimental therapies which have not been approved by the Food and Drug Administration.

SSDI - Social Security Disability Insurance is a federal insurance program of the United States government, funded by payroll tax and designed to provide monthly benefits to people who have a medically determinable disability that restricts their ability to be employed.

ACKNOWLEDGMENTS

BARKAN, Ady: "What I Refuse to Accept with Serenity." This article first appeared in a November 2018 issue of *The Nation* magazine.

FANOUS, Angelina: "Divine Intervention." A version of this article first appeared as "I Traveled to Egypt for a Miracle Cure for My ALS" in a March 2015 issue of *VICE* magazine.

HOOVER, Shelly: Four Pieces. These originally appeared on the author's website blog, at www.shellyhoover.com.

MACISAAC, Norman: "See What Others Can't." This excerpt first appeared in the memoir *The Best of the Worst News: Tales of Inspiration from Around the World and My Life with ALS* published by Insomniac Press, 2019.

POLEN, Corey: "A Hoosier ALS Journey." These entries first appeared on the author's blog and at www.gofundme.com/f/standforcorey.

SMITH, Jay: "Divorce or Death? A Real Life Decision", "The Cost of ALS is Killing Us and Our Vets" and "Man With ALS Wants to Be Turned Into a Robot" were first published in *Huffington Post*.

THOMSON, Michael: "Mooncake" and "The Train." These first appeared in *Forum*, the City College of San Francisco literary magazine, in 2011.

VALOR, Eric: Three Poems. These also appear in the author's collection *Hamachi Eyes* (2018). The poems "My Strings Sing for Renaissance" and "Iki & Etta" was first published in *Queen Mob's Tea House*. The poem "Locked-In Blues" first appeared in *The New England Review of Books*.

WALLACH, Brian: "My Story." This excerpt was originally published as "Brian's Story" on the I AM ALS website, www.iamals.org/brians-story.

SPECIAL THANKS to Paul Rowe, who served as a liaison to the ALS community throughout the editorial and production processes; to Tianna G. Hansen, for her role in the initial realization of this anthology in print; and Zachary Bos of Pen & Anvil, for his meticulous, sensitive editorial assistance.

DEDICATED TO
THE MEMORY OF ERIC VALOR
AND TO ALL OTHERS WHO
HAVE BEEN TOUCHED BY
THIS DISEASE.

NORMAN MACISAAC

See What Others Can't: Leap into a Parallel World

The following excerpt is from the author's book, The Best of the Worst News: Tales of Inspiration from Around the World and My Life with ALS *(Insomniac Press, 2019). MacIsaac was diagnosed in 2014, and has since traveled extensively, visiting five continents. "Travel is life-affirming," he explains. "I love to travel; but it's about more than traveling. It's about living life to the fullest and focusing on the positive, on the 'awful lot to live for' that Lou Gehrig referred to in his iconic speech." - Eds.*

SHORTLY AFTER RECEIVING MY WORST NEWS, MY WIFE AND I sat down to write our bucket lists. A lot of our entries were identical, including an African safari and a trip to Italy. Although I have travelled all of my life, I've often failed to seize opportunities. For instance, Christine and I had been planning a trip to Italy for decades but never made it happen. We had planned a Kenyan safari before I was diagnosed, but we had to call it off because our son fell ill.

This was special. Bucket list travel has an unrivalled level of intensity and a heightened sense of *carpe diem*. And, for me, there was one unexpected discovery: Traveling with a disability is challenging, but it can also be more rewarding. It will open your eyes to a different perspective on the world—a world you hadn't seen before. Join me as I leap into a parallel world, where I saw invisible people and my new needs translated into the opportunity to see the best humankind has to offer.

It was the summer of 2016, and we embarked on yet another bucket list trip that took us to Kenya and then Italy.

First, allow me to pose this question: Why do we travel anymore? You can see remote locations through Google Maps and Google Earth, see the best images in documentaries filmed in stunning HD, and probably learn more than any tourist guide can ever tell you by reading online information at your leisure or watching YouTube videos for free.

Travel isn't about what we see or the photos and information we gather. It's about experience. It's about the unique feeling you get in places. It's about sounds and smells. It's about the way people talk. It's about that veal tortellini that melts in your mouth. The travel experience is about seeing things that catch your eye and that stimulate your imagination rather than the images that documentary filmmakers spoon-feed you, regardless of how amazing they are compared to yours.

In Kenya, when I first entered Masai Mara Natural Reserve, it wasn't a lion or a rhino that triggered something in me but a simple lone acacia tree that stood in defiance, punctuating the crisp line of the horizon where fields of grasslands met the pale blue sky. Umbrella thorn acacia trees are nature's parasols. They create oases of shade in the savanna. Yet the trunk of this one was gnarled. It was as though it had cowered under the blazing sun, leaning to the left before it resolutely spread its branches out to create a light-green canopy and cast its precious shade.

As I grabbed on tight while the van I was riding in dipped and rocked over this bumpy trail, that was my moment with that tree amid tall straw-colored grass stroked by gentle winds. It was a moment that was mine alone.

The travel experience goes even deeper though. More than the animals I saw, the pasta I devoured, and the sights I visited, my travel experience plunged me into a reality and connected me with people as I would have never imagined before.

Given my new and growing mobility challenges, I faced obstacles and frustrations when visiting over rough terrain and cobblestones. But amid the challenge was a world few have ever entered, so bear with me as I take you along a pathway of determination over disheartenment into the bitter-sweet reality that you may only perceive if you dare take the time and make the effort to peer into our world. This is not a travel journal of my safari and my trip to Italy; it's about my inner journey and the world of reduced mobility.

Christine was busy carrying the remaining pieces of luggage downstairs, and I stopped to sit down in front of the symbols of my new reality as one who was and still is determined to stay active. I stared at the new rollator/transport chair. A year ago, I didn't even know what a rollator or a transport chair was. Now I was the not-so-proud owner of a hybrid model that combined the two. A rollator is basically a walker with four wheels, and a transport chair is a lightweight wheelchair. This model, the Airgo Fusion, easily converts into a chair for use at airports, museums, or shopping centers, or whenever I'm confronted with long distances that surpass my abilities. A flip and a couple of switches and, voilà, this rollator becomes a chair that my caregiver can push. This new purchase would serve as my travelling wheelchair on this trip.

I used to be the one to carry the suitcases up and down the stairs. No more. There I sat at the bottom, damning the finely designed equipment that screamed out to me and everyone else the extent of my mobility challenges. It used to be just a cane.

I then started using one Canadian crutch (two in icy conditions—with five-pronged ice grips). I gradually learned to use the wheelchair service at airports. I then finally procured my own wheelchair. For nearly a year, I resisted the recommendation of my physiotherapist and occupational therapist to use a rollator, or wheeled walker. I refused to even try one. I must have appeared stubborn to my occupational therapist, but it wasn't stubbornness. It was fear and pride with a healthy dose of sadness and regret.

In the end, though, the multiple falls and the scar on my nose proved me wrong. So, as I planned a trip that included obstacles ranging from uneven, unpaved terrain in parts of Africa to cobblestones in Europe, I finally gave in and purchased a rollator/transport chair. As necessary as all of these mobility aids were, they represented my inevitable decline into a world of limitations. The Canadian crutches were the first adjustment after the cane, but the rollator was the hardest. One might think that the wheelchair would be the biggest hurdle, but, for me, the wheeled walker was the ultimate symbol of advanced old age, used by decrepit old souls as they hunched over and moved so painfully slow that you wished someone would just put them in a wheelchair.

At the young age of fifty-two, I exhaled a breath of total disheartenment in the face of these new mobility aids on which I was growing increasingly dependent. I should have been grateful that I could still travel, still work—albeit at an increasingly slower pace—and still walk short distances with some support. I should have been rejoicing that my breathing was not yet affected and that my voice, that had weakened considerably in June, was actually doing slightly better. But I wasn't.

I instead felt like I was sinking—sinking into a new reality that I silently scorned. *This was not the way I traveled,* I told myself. I was an adventurer. I was spontaneous. I walked swiftly through airports and strolled through new cities with my head held high, admiring the sights, the sounds, and the architecture. But no more. I now had to plan and search for accessible routes. I traveled with mobility aids. It took great concentration for me to walk, so I couldn't look around like I used to. I instead had to focus on navigating sidewalks and carefully making my way down from the curb and back up again on the other side.

I had been forced into this new reality by an ailment that appeared out of nowhere, with no rhyme or reason, and I damned those innovative mobility aids as the guardians of my new reality. I wanted to break them into a million pieces, cancel my trip, and curl up into a ball. I felt cornered, stuck between the rational desire to go ahead with my trip and the resentment and despair over everything I had lost.

SOMETHING GNU

A week later, across the Atlantic and just south of the equator, my attention shifted outward to nature's spectacle. Around me, a growing number of gnu (pronounced the same as *new*), or wildebeest, amassed before my eyes, moaning nervously in anticipation of their upcoming challenge.

Hundreds of wildebeest had gathered next to the river while thousands more formed lines, rushing toward the river from multiple directions in the vicinity. Eventually, a couple of the beasts ventured down the dusty path toward the river and then returned, ostensibly having determined that the crossing was too treacherous. Either they had found the path down too steep or they feared the presence of predators nearby—lions, leopards, or hyenas positioned along the riverbank, or crocodiles in the water, lurking patiently in anticipation of an upcoming feast.

The wildebeest kicked up the sand as they returned fearfully from the riverbank, sending a cloud of dust into the air. As the size of the herd grew and increasing numbers congregated near the river, the pressure to cross became palpable.

If you don't know what a wildebeest looks like—and in this case, in the Masai Mara region of southern Kenya, I am referring to the migratory blue wildebeest—it looks like a strange mythical creature a child could have drawn. Technically, it's an antelope, but it looks a lot like a nervous cow with smaller hindquarters compared to their forequarters, a long black face with short horns, a white beard, and the mane and tail of a horse.

They moaned and bleated as the herd swelled near the river. Then a few zebras joined in and headed bravely down the riverbank. We watched this and hoped the wildebeest would follow, but we knew that sometimes they don't cross at all, opting instead to return to grazing. Eventually, though, pressure would grow, as nearly all the grass nearby had been eaten or trampled. They would leave the landscape looking like it was the scene of an epic outdoor rock concert, minus the litter that humans normally leave behind. Fortunately for the Serengeti and the Masai Mara, all the wildebeest leave behind is well-distributed organic fertilizer that will help prepare the land for the next season of the wildebeests' favorite grass.

Mostly, though, this build-up culminates in a massive frenetic crossing, triggered by just a few trailblazing wildebeest, or perhaps by following proactive zebras, who dare take the leap. Since the riverbank is often quite steep and the herd pushes from behind relentlessly, those descending to the river have no choice but to take the plunge.

Finally, it happened. As the numbers increased, the wildebeest careered off the embankment into the river below. It was as if the higher and longer the wildebeest jumped into the river, the farther and higher those that followed sprang. The resulting event was of Olympic grandeur, with thousands of five-foot-tall animals weighing up to 270 kilograms (600 pounds) hurtling into the river, rustling across, and struggling to make it back up the other side.

This was all part of the annual great migration of the Serengeti and Masai Mara, a natural phenomenon that a panel of six judges in *USA Today* voted as one of the "New Seven Wonders." What impressed me were the group dynamics that could bring a herd of fearful moaning ungulates to leap into crocodile-infested waters, while hungry cats waited nearby, hoping to snatch their latest meal.

CROSSING THAT RIVER

I sometimes felt like the wildebeest, compelled to make (or coerced into making) those dangerous crossings by the forces of nature. Acquiescing to multiple adaptations, overwhelmed by compound and overlapping challenges, I followed medical advice and gradually found myself living by the prescriptions written for me.

For some time, I found myself resisting the calls of occupational therapists and physiotherapists to do this or that or to prepare for the next inevitable phase. Yet, in the end, the forces of nature proved them right. After multiple falls, a minor concussion, and a lasting scar, I finally gave in and belatedly followed their advice. Despite my pigheadedness, I have been congratulated for my courage and my determination, but I often doubt my merit. I'm just like the wildebeest, I would say to myself, pressured into the inevitable cliff dive that looks brave but really isn't.

Perhaps I'm not giving the wildebeest the credit they deserve. They might appear doltish and damned to follow, but there might just be a method to their madness. For one, the migration has proven its effectiveness for thousands of years, and these so-called "blue wildebeest" are thriving. Second, the strong instinct to stick together protects them from predators, as if their DNA constantly reminds them that united they stand and divided they fall. Third, they somehow manage to communicate and are attentive to warning signs from other animals, such as baboons. Finally, while they might appear to be consummate followers, they can also be seen doubling back across the perilous river to retrieve their offspring that strayed among the frenzy. In short, these are certainly not the most intelligent creatures on the east African plains, but they are survivors that are too easily underestimated by human observers and predators alike.

So there's no shame in being a survivor like the wildebeest, I told myself. But there was more to it because this trip, this metaphorical river crossing, was neither an annual event imprinted in my DNA nor a case of simply doing what needed to be done. I didn't have to travel, just as I didn't have to continue finding ways to keep on working. I wasn't following the herd; I was defying it. I wasn't reacting; I was being proactive.

The very tools that I cursed became my allies in the struggle to overcome my new physical challenges. In the process, rather than staying home and moaning and bleating with the herd, I'd actually increased the challenges I would face. I wasn't travelling with the mainstream herd; rather, I was in another group entirely in the parallel world of mobility challenges.

Before December 2014, I knew nothing of this world. I didn't notice the army of wheelchair warriors pushing the elderly and the disabled through airports around the globe. I hadn't given much thought to how wheelchair-bound passengers got on the plane or down the narrow aisle to their seat. But then I became the one transported separately on

Photos from July 2016. Top to bottom: A wildebeest (gnu) dives into the Mara River in Kenya (credit: N. MacIsaac). Wildebeest dash toward the river (credit: Marie-Christine Tremblay). Wildebeest crossing the Mara (credit: N. MacIsaac). Norman walks along the coast north of Kilifi with the aid of Canadian crutches (credit: Nicholas Trent).

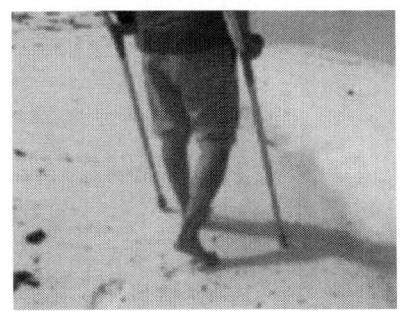

and off the plane, often embarking first and deplaning last, taking elevators rather than escalators, and being transported by a special lift from the plane instead of taking the stairs.

With this world came challenges but also unique opportunities for interaction. Christine spent hours researching and planning how to overcome these obstacles, and every day this was combined with countless unexpected hurdles. Together, we defied the limits of what I was supposed to be able to do, knowing full well we would be frequently frustrated but also often equally surprised by the heartwarming acts of kindness along the way.

For instance, I shouldn't have been surprised when a taxi driver in Rome dropped us off—a fifty-four-year-old petite blonde and her physically challenged partner—at a place where a flight of stairs separated us from the Coliseum. By the time we realized this, the taxi was long gone, and we found ourselves staring down at a formidable adversary. Built from centuries-old stones, these stairs were steep, uneven, and narrow, and there was no handrail to hold onto for the last few yards. At this point, we froze like two wildebeest confronted by the steep riverbank leading to crocodile-infested waters. I looked at Christine and then at the stairs, and then I contemplated going back up and around. As we assessed our predicament, a swarm of tourists made their way around us.

It was as though time had stopped and the world was passing us by until a sturdy gentleman appeared and offered to help. His muscular arms were the size of my calves, and his footing was sure. In a soothing voice, he told me to take all the time I needed. My left leg quivered and hesitated as I negotiated each step, but his arm was steady. Propped up by Christine on one hand and this stranger on the other, I made my way downstairs slowly while he coached me on.

As I paused between challenging steps, he told me how he had struggled to walk for three years after his accident. Then, as I resumed and conquered yet another step, he celebrated my victory over each one. "The stairs will not win," he told me. And he was right.

We experienced countless other moments like this one. At the Vatican Museums, we encountered unexpected steps as Christine wheeled me along. Having exerted considerable energy pushing me up to that point and struggling to find the accessible route, she once again just stopped. This time, the reaction was almost instantaneous as a quartet of Vatican visitors reached for the four corners of my transport chair and hoisted me to the next level, scarcely leaving us the time to thank them.

If you observe closely when you travel, you might notice wheelchair lifts, ramps, and other special equipment and services for the physically challenged at airports and museums. What you won't see is whether these services are efficient or even functional. During our trip in Italy, for instance, accessibility was imperfect, inconsistent, and unreliable. The infrastructure we saw was often window dressing, and either it didn't work or nobody knew how to operate it. With the information being either insufficient or imperfect, we were constantly asking questions and preparing for disappointment.

Unlike the wildebeest, humans have developed complex communication systems, technical innovations (i.e. tools, machines, and systems), and norms to overcome the obstacles of the mobility challenged. Yet, in the end, this is not where our humanity shines through. Technology and communication are undependable, and bureaucracy and apathy are often our foes. Despite our so-called superiority, we often end up relying on the same support systems that work in the animal kingdom because when technology and systems fail, all we have to fall back on are our fellow human beings.

Another challenge was my invisibility. At the Coliseum in Rome, a French tourist tripped over my crutches as he scrambled to find his way. As he fell, he was about to swear at the obstacle in his way when he realized it was a man with crutches and a leg brace just trying to remain standing. On several occasions, tourists admiring artwork—their eyes transfixed on the works of Raphael or Michelangelo—almost ended up in my lap as they collided with my transport chair.

At Castel Sant'Angelo, while Christine headed up the stairs to explore the parts of this medieval castle that were inaccessible to me, I sat and looked around. I took the time to enjoy the view of the Passetto di Borgo, a half-mile-long walkway linking the Vatican to the castle. It was built by Pope Nicholas III in 1277 and even served as an escape route for popes on two occasions.

As crowds passed by, I looked at the fading frescoes on the ceiling and then at the people around me. Sitting in a wheelchair next to an elderly gentleman was a boy of about ten with his tongue slightly sticking out. Both he and the elderly man beside him looked tired and bored. I sat and observed. This was not the Italy in any guidebook, nor was this a scene that most others would even notice.

Christine took more time than I had expected, so I sat quietly observing harried tourists and enthusiastic travelers as they passed by. Few took notice of me unless my crutches impeded their path. Probably fewer took note of the boy in the wheelchair and the elderly gentleman.

After some time, Christine descended with a camera full of pictures of the sights she had seen, and we gradually made our way to the elevator. Waiting there was the boy in the wheelchair, the elderly man—who I now understood to be the boy's grandfather—and a woman who appeared to be the boy's mother. I explained that we needed to find a staff member with the key to the elevator, and Christine departed on a quest to find him. The boy looked at me as his mother put her camera back into her purse. "I'm also going to wait for my wife's pictures to see what's up there," I told him. His mother smiled in a way that said thank you with her eyes.

Christine and the attendant arrived to unlock the elevator, and the mother then looked at her son and said, "He also had to wait while his wife was visiting, and we'll also look at the photos together." The message was simple: He was not alone. Nobody else seemed to pay any heed to their situation, but we had met in that parallel universe unseen by all others, where we waited to see the pictures of the places beyond our reach.

When we travel, we see all sorts of things. On safari, we were constantly amazed by nature's spectacle all around us. In Italy, we stared in wonder at the ceiling of the Sistine Chapel and were enchanted by the exquisite landscapes of Tuscany. Christine and I took countless pictures, trying to find the angle and frame that represented our unique view and experience.

Beneath this level of observation, though, was a more profound travel experience where we gained new perspectives as well as a few precious moments where we truly connected with others. Mine was that moment with the unnamed boy in the wheelchair and his caregiver. His mother appreciated my comment of solidarity, and I appreciated her need to visit and experience things beyond the physical limitations of her son.

I understood her fatigue and her need to see areas of the castle that were inaccessible to her son because she oughtn't be limited by his constraints. She cherished those precious moments where she lived for herself despite her situation. For her, I'm sure my simple affirmation validated her time alone on the inaccessible level of the castle. For me, it made me reflect on the new club I had involuntarily joined: the club of the physically challenged. It was a beautiful, poignant moment. I connected with another human being who probably would have remained invisible to me had destiny not decided we would share certain challenges.

Despite countless obstacles and limitations, it was an unforgettable July of new sights and cherished memories, but the one experience I had to share was a world unseen by most: the world of the physically challenged, their caregivers, their friends, and good Samaritans. I encourage you to make the extra effort to look for it and to seek opportunities to interact with those who live in it. The next time you take the stairs or tread effortlessly up one or two steps to enter your favorite shop or restaurant, ask yourself, "Where are those for whom this is an insurmountable barrier or those who cannot read these signs if they're not in braille?" Then extend this beyond physical limitations to understand those facing depression and other forms of mental illness, the homeless, or any other marginalized people. Let's call it a quest to understand and learn about invisible parallel worlds. &.

: ADAPT :
:: SURVIVE ::
: PREVAIL :

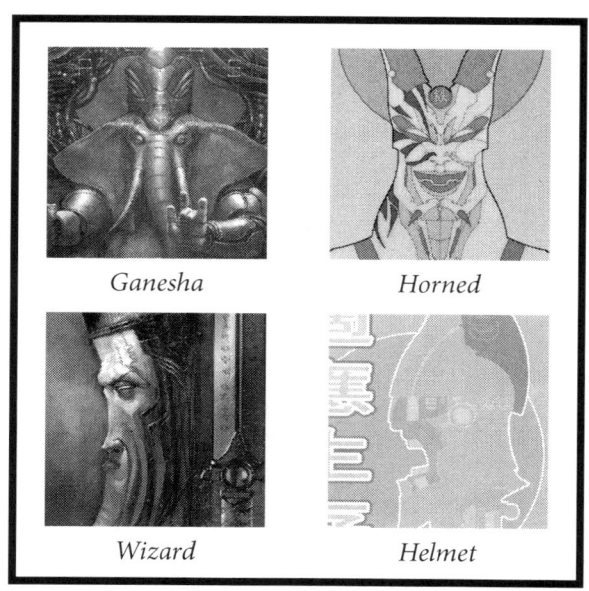

Ganesha

Horned

Wizard

Helmet

AN ART PORTFOLIO
BY FRANCIS TSAI

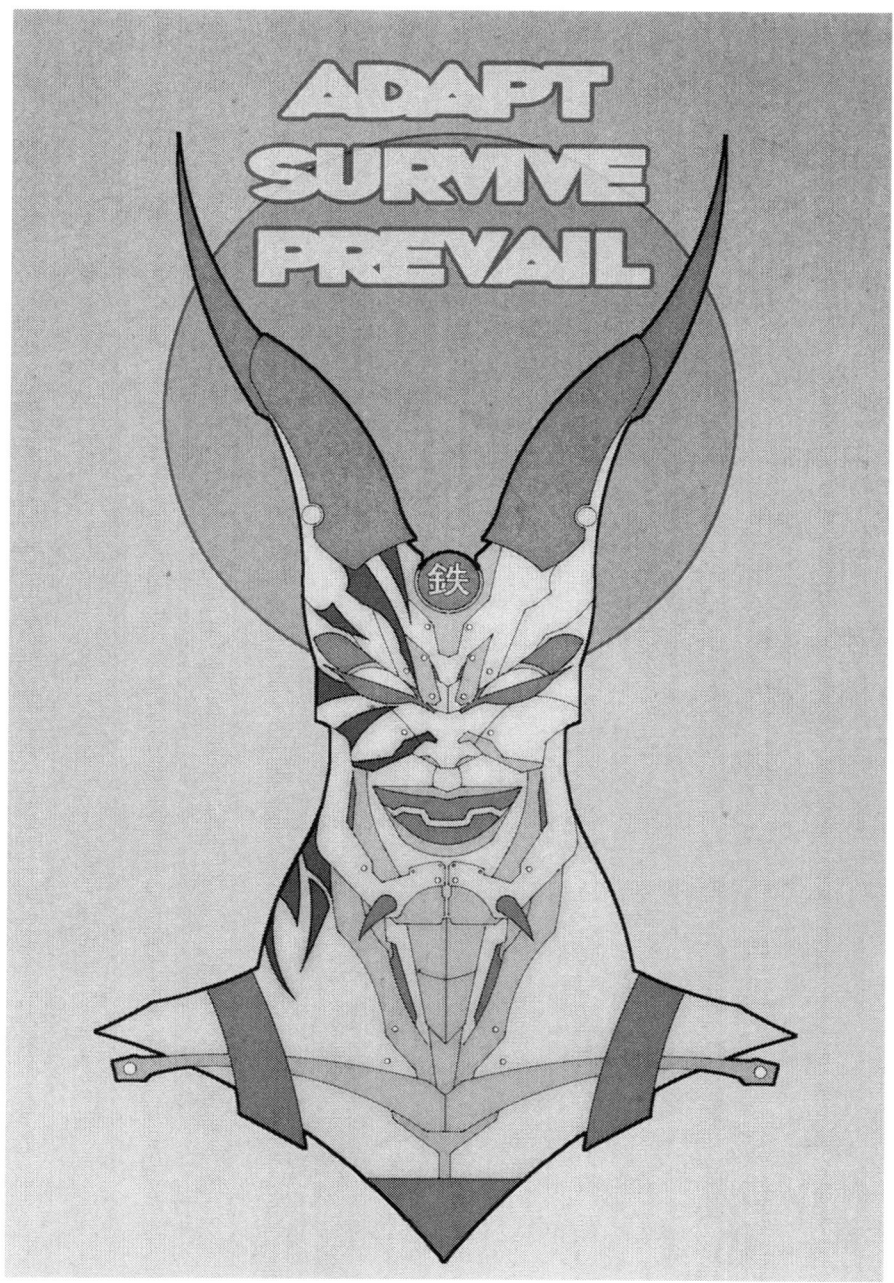

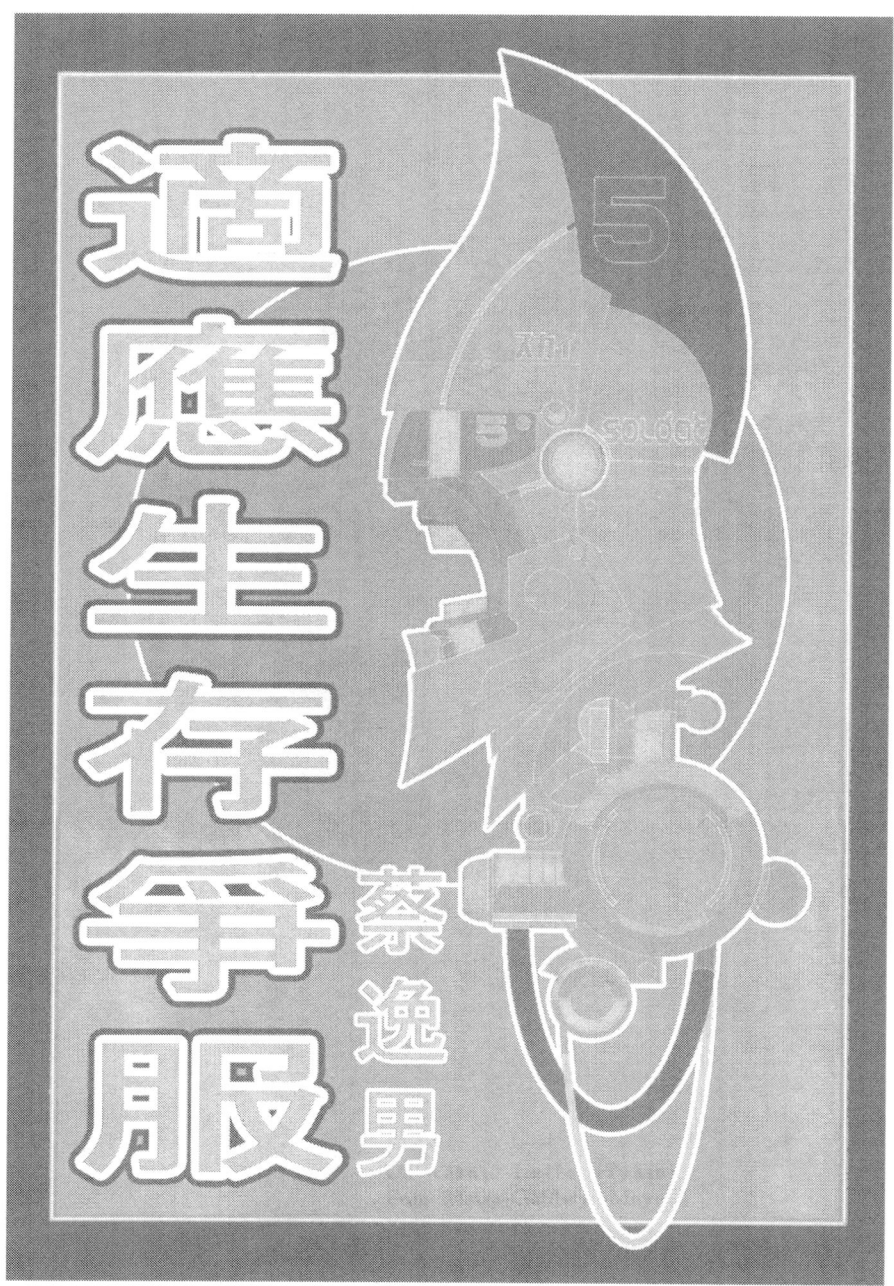

適應生存爭服 蔡逸男

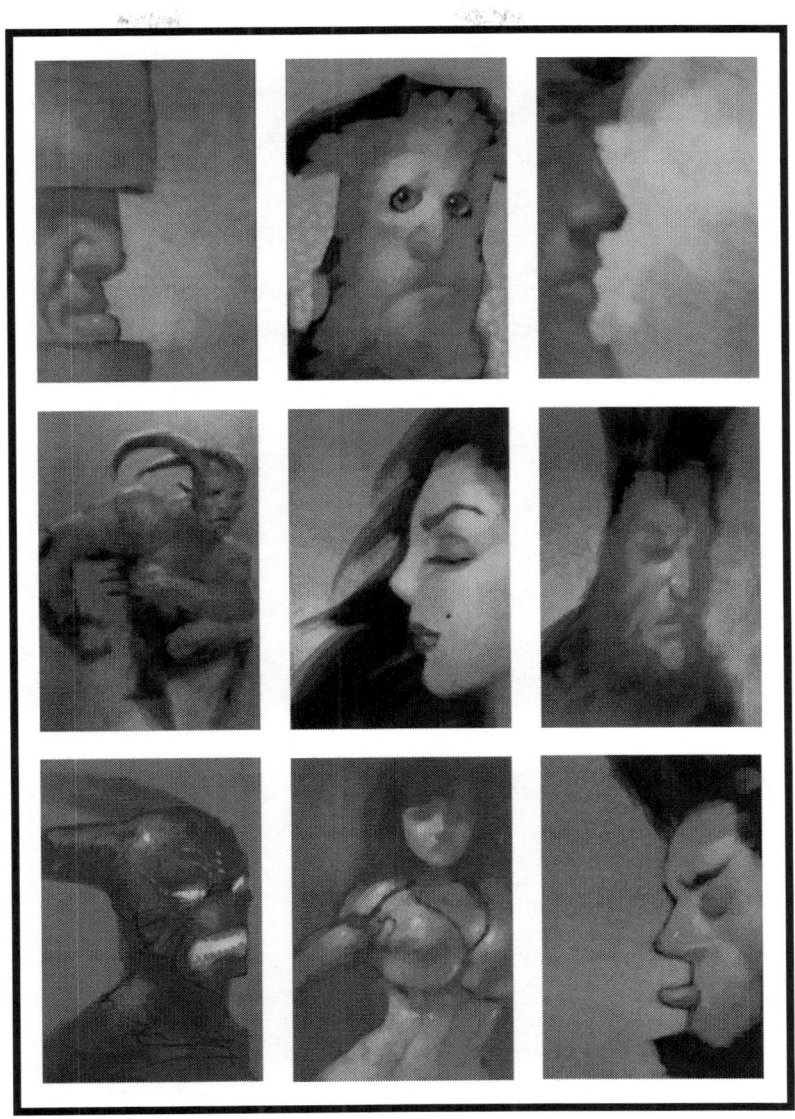

FIND MORE OF TSAI'S ART AT TEAMGT.COM

DAVID O'NAN

Fever 32

I am aware of light above me
Unaware of the darkness that is eating away inside of me
Then I look at my family
Why are they full of tears?
Why has my body defeated me?
When my mind is still young
God saved me thirty-four years before
Now he needs me ❧

BRIAN WALLACH

My Story

THIS IS AN ALS STORY. IT HAPPENS TO BE MY STORY. BUT IT could be your story. Your spouse's story. Your child's story.

I was diagnosed with ALS in November 2017. I was thirty-seven.

With two girls under three. And I was told then that this disease will take my life. Rob my daughters of their father. And my wife of her husband. That, however, is not how my story will end. Why? Because, together we are going to cure ALS.

The first time I heard the words "ALS" from my doctors was on August 14, 2017. As those words crashed around her office, my family and I asked questions. Trying desperately to make sense of this diagnosis. Wasn't I too young to have ALS? How could I have it if we have no family history of ALS? Aren't there parts of my symptoms that suggest something else, anything else?

The answers didn't come that day. There is not yet a test to diagnosis someone with ALS. Instead, it is a diagnosis that is reached when all other options are exhausted. What doctors call a diagnosis by exclusion. And as we were waiting for that diagnosis we read everything we could find about ALS.

Let me start with the punchline: there is no cure right now for ALS. Every 4.4 minutes someone in the world is diagnosed with ALS. Every 4.4 minutes someone dies of ALS. In the time it takes you to read this document someone's son will have been diagnosed with ALS and someone's mother will have died from ALS.

ALS is a disease that turns your body against itself. It causes your body to attack itself. To wear out its muscles until you can no longer move your hands. Your arms. Your legs. Eat. And ultimately breathe.

Lou Gehrig had ALS; so did Stephen Hawking. So do nearly five hundred thousand people around the world. One out of every five hundred Americans will be diagnosed with ALS. Those diagnosed are young and old, male and female, and every skin color. ALS doesn't discriminate. It can affect anyone. Ninety percent of the people diagnosed with ALS have no family history of the disease. On average, they will live two to five years after being given this diagnosis.

So, this story, my story, is actually our story—because if ALS can affect anyone, curing it takes everyone. The good news is that our story can have a happy ending. That's because ALS is not an incurable disease; it is an underfunded one. Indeed, even though ALS research is badly underfunded, researchers are closer to finding a cure than ever before having identified over forty genes connected to ALS. In fact, the tools are in place to defeat ALS.

The ALS community has the necessary building blocks of a movement for a cure: patients, advocates, and organizations striving for new recognition, new commitments, and new breakthroughs. They remain hopeful, driven, inspiring, and inspired. What is missing from the fight right now is a patient-led, patient-centric movement that can empower those in the fight and bring those not affected by the disease into our struggle. So that's what we have built with I AM ALS: a patient-led, patient-centric movement that will drive collaboration, build and provide critical missing resources for the ALS community, organize and empower the ALS community, and drive increased awareness of ALS in order to generate millions of dollars in new funding to accelerate finding a cure.

Thank you for joining us—the patients, caregivers, advocates, and doctors at the helm of I AM ALS—in this fight. As I sit here typing these words, I am filled with hope because I truly believe that I will live to see a cure for ALS. A cure that will allow me to raise my girls with my wife. To be there for the father-daughter wedding dance. A cure that will change the lives of tens of thousands by ensuring that no patient ever has to be told, "you have ALS, get your affairs in order."

We will win this fight, and when we do we will unlock critical breakthroughs that will help defeat Parkinson's, Alzheimer's, Frontal Temporal Dementia, and beyond. Saving the lives of an estimated one hundred and thirty-five million people who would have been killed by these diseases.

This is our dream at I AM ALS. Like all dreams, it is reality mixed with hope. We will find a cure. That part is the reality. The dream is doing it in the next three years, not in twenty years.

So, will you dream with us? ❧

HOLLY COOPER

Eighteen Months

YOU CALL ME ON THE THIRD DAY OF FEBRUARY. I NEED YOUR help with something, you say. You rarely ask for help so I know this is not nothing.

I'm having trouble with my arms, you say. I have this machine that might help but I can't hook it up to my shoulders. You take a breath. They say I have motor neuron disease.

I'm sitting on a bench by the lake. There's a vacuum in my ears as the world goes silent. Like a bomb just went off so close I couldn't hear it.

Come over, I tell you. I help you with the electrical muscle stimulation machine you bought off Craigslist, place the leads onto your bony shoulders that used to be covered with bulging muscles. As the thing buzzes, your shoulders hike up into a sort of involuntary shrug, over and over. I don't know, you say, to make me laugh. I don't know.

Your upper arms don't work at all. Even your tattoos have shrunk. I wonder how you've been getting dressed, showering, eating. You're downplaying it, but I know you're scared. I know you. Move in with me, I say.

No one at the VA actually told you—you read it on the discharge papers they handed you on your way out after your last appointment. Final diagnosis: motor neuron disease.

You tell me about how, after you left the VA that day, you went to Ocean Beach. You sat there looking out at the Pacific, thinking, if this is for real, I should end it now. Spare everyone this nightmare. As you sat there, a crow landed near you and began to hop around, circling you in the sand.

The VA is wrong, we decide.

We get the CD with your MRI scans and read them ourselves. Your field medic training is still paying off twenty years on. See, you say, pointing, right there. A narrowing on the left side of your cervical spine. Cervical radiculopathy. Pinched nerves, that's got to be it. Because the alternative is unthinkable.

But seven weeks later, after one EMG and then another—the mantra *please let it be cancer* playing in our heads—it's confirmed. You have probable-to-definite ALS, the neurologist says flatly. She attempts a lighthearted remark about Stephen Hawking that does not land well.

That night, we hold on to each other like we're drowning and stare saucer-eyed into the darkness. We'll do this countless times over the coming months.

We start researching. When you can't sleep, which is often, you sit up till 4:00 AM reading everything you can find online. When I'm supposed to be working, I'm Googling like a madwoman. There must be something out there, something these doctors have overlooked. It's astounding what we'll believe, given our usual skepticism—the stunning lack of evidence that we fail to see whenever we read about this treatment in Thailand, that special diet, this supplement that supposedly reversed one man's symptoms.

You have your third EMG in April. A second opinion from the neurology department at a respected civilian hospital. We're still clinging to the cliffside with two fingers, hopeful that the VA missed something, but the diagnosis is the same. They shoot down everything we've found in our research, they look at us with patience and sadness. They've heard all of this before.

People diagnosed with ALS live on average two to five years, all the websites and doctors say.

We've transferred your care to this hospital because it's one of six sites running a clinical trial. Autologous mesenchymal stem cells, administered intrathecally—meaning they extract your own stem cells, sprinkle fairy dust on them to make them grow, then inject them back into your spinal fluid. Phase three, very promising. I'm going to be a medical miracle, you say. I'm going to be on the cover of *TIME* with the others who are the first in history to beat this.

The trial has a one-to-one placebo. We know this is how science has always worked. We refuse to consider the possibility that you'll be one of the unlucky ones who get only saline solution.

We devour the phase two data and anecdotes. We talk to the wife of a man who participated in phase two. Like you, he had lost the use of his arms. After one injection he could actually shampoo his own hair again.

Imagine.

You'd do anything to have your arms back for even one day. We choose not to think about the part where phase two ended and his progression returned and he lost his arms all over again, along with everything else.

We quickly learn about ALS clinic, how demoralizing and exhausting and pointless it feels. Just a long day of endless assessments and suggestions for how to give way to the monster as it invades your body. All they do is chart my demise, you say.

We throw all our hope into the clinical trial.

In May you have to stop driving. It crushes your spirit in a way that even giving up surfing and playing guitar didn't come close to.

You never want to go out in public. You're self-conscious about your body and having to be fed. You can't even stand to have the blinds open. A beautiful sunny day, singing birds, laughing voices feel like an insult. It hurts you to see healthy people doing normal things and the world carrying on without you.

We still try to laugh. It's our thing, or it was anyway. We watch stand-up and *The Office*. It's surreal how many jokes there are about death and dying, how I never noticed this before.

My birthday. I come home from work to find that you've made me a cake. A double-layer cake, my name written in frosting. I stare at you, speechless. This means you had gone to the store, picked the ingredients off the shelf, went through the line, had to ask the clerk for help handing the money over and getting the bags into your hands. Tears are rolling down my face. What? You say, like it was nothing.

You can't listen to music anymore. It used to be everything to you, but now it causes you physical pain—the memories, the emotions you used to feel that you don't have access to anymore.

You have no appetite, and you start to have trouble swallowing. Chewing is exhausting. Eating is a chore. But you push through every meal with the same determination that you previously used to bench two-fifty.

When I buy groceries, I wonder if you'll be alive by the expiration dates.

July. We drive seven hours south and report for your clinical trial appointment, the last one before you're officially admitted into the trial (assuming your progression rate isn't too slow, or too fast). I'm so sorry, the coordinator says, there's been a delay. Everyone in the trial will be at a standstill for two months. Two more months of doing nothing to try to fight this beast, two more months of losses.

Two months would turn out to be one-sixth of your remaining life.

As a backup plan, we start fundraising to travel to South Korea. They're doing something similar over there, and the expensive treatment is available commercially even as it goes through its own clinical trial. This would never happen in the U.S.

In August you have fall number three, on the sidewalk. We're walking to your car in the dark, your toe catches a crack. You go down hard, flat onto your face with a sickening crunch. You are unresponsive, a pool of blood forming under your head while I sob my way through the 911 call.

They take you to Highland Hospital as a trauma level two. I follow the ambulance. As I approach your room in the ER, I can hear you cracking jokes and making everyone laugh, and I let myself breathe again. Your face is torn and swollen, like someone beat you without mercy. You've only fractured a cheekbone; the rest will heal. Later you try to make light of it, tell friends you tripped on an ant.

The blood stain will remain on the sidewalk for nine months.

When we go to bed at night, as your body twitches, I can feel electricity buzzing from your muscles into my skin. You confess how afraid you are. You tell me things you'll never tell anyone else.

You start to talk about your exit plan.

The choking starts. Every once in a while, when you drink water or eat something too dry or doughy. We know it will only get worse.

By November, you're having trouble transferring in and out of chairs, getting off the toilet. Suddenly you need help sitting up and getting out of bed. But the most terrifying part is your breathing is now affected.

One evening, you shuffle outside for some air. I hear a heavy thud and I know you've fallen, that your head hit the concrete. Thankfully you're okay, but I'm still hysterical, even though I am not that person. Maybe I am now.

It's finally time for your first spinal injection in the clinical trial, and we're scared but excited. To have a chance means everything, even if it's one in a million. As your sister and I wheel you into the oncology ward where they'll do the procedure, we hear Johnny Mathis singing "Chances Are." You had it queued up on your phone just for this moment.

In your room, your sister and I are asked to leave while the doctors do the procedure. An hour feels like weeks. When we return, there's a light in your eyes that wasn't there before. We sit with you, help you eat lunch, pretending that we're not all waiting for a miracle to materialize before our eyes.

I don't know if it's my imagination, you say, but I feel like I can breathe a little better. Could it be that you're finally going to get a break? There's a flutter in my chest. This must be what hope feels like.

Back at home, we keep watching and waiting. You swear you can turn a doorknob more easily that you could before.

But that's it. Soon your breathing feels like it did before, and turning a doorknob doesn't seem like a big deal. The hope fades and disintegrates at our feet. We go back to preparing for South Korea, decide to go ahead with the next infusion in January and hope a second dose will do something.

In early December you fall backward onto the carpet. You're unhurt, but your mom and I can't get you up. We call 911 and two burly firemen pick you up and set you in a chair as if you're a doll. You don't say a word but I know you're humiliated. You used to be the muscle-bound first responder helping others.

Your legs are getting thinner. The fronts of your shin bones are razor sharp. You can't negotiate even a single stair. The next treatment for the clinical trial is in days, and I don't know how I'm going to get you from the car into the hotel and then to the hospital the next morning. I rent a transport chair from a medical supply place—the local "donor closet" has none. You just look at me with defeat.

You still insist on walking as much as possible, but I'm always scared. The floors are hard as concrete in our new apartment. I follow you around with my arms out. As if I could catch you.

Your sister comes down to live with us. This is no longer a one-person job. She loves you, she makes you laugh. She is a godsend. I'm so relieved and grateful even as we all struggle to adapt to our new roles and this new life in a town where none of us wants to be. There are some tensions, misunderstandings. My ego is fragile.

It's becoming apparent that it's too late for South Korea. You can't possibly make the long trips or lie flat on your back after the treatments.

We're at the VA, you're being fitted for your power wheelchair. The rep chats cheerfully at no one as she works, while the morose woman from Prosthetics sits staring and we're hunched over in the corner holding hands. In the shadow of your Astros cap, tears are falling silently down your cheeks. I lean over and wipe them away. No one else notices.

The real pain starts in early January. Not just muscle cramps like before. Your shrinking muscles are tearing as they're being stretched on the bone. The neurologist looks at us blankly. ALS is not supposed to involve pain. She is caring, but she doesn't have time to become a specialist in ALS. She starts you on oxycodone. This fits nicely into your exit plan. You try to bear the pain and take as few pills as possible, squirrel away the rest. You're more and more desperate to have an out.

Now you need help with every aspect of toileting. Bathing has become difficult and dangerous. Eventually even your sister is helping you with the most personal of tasks. She loves you with a fierce dedication that I have never witnessed in anyone, let alone siblings.

The wheelchair is ready in early February—exactly a year after that phone call, when you first told me you were sick. As we leave the VA, you speed down the hall, driving exactly as you drove a car: Scary-fast but skillful.

That night you go for a solo ride around the apartment complex. I'm relieved that you can at least feel some shred of independence. I worry that you won't come back.

It's your forty-eighth birthday. It will be your last. We all know it. We sing to you in the candlelight, our voices trembling through our smiles. One by one we falter as something catches in our throats. Your sister runs out the door into the night.

Later, as everyone is saying goodbye, you have fall number eight when you crash backward into the coffee table. It leaves a bruise like a large eggplant. You wear it like a badge.

You and I have been sleeping in the queen bed in the extra room, trying to be a normal couple. But it's getting harder for you to breathe, and the room is too small for your wheelchair to get very far. The hospital bed sits waiting for this moment in the other room. It's just one more defeat, a surrender of yet another border to the enemy. In our new room, I pull the inflatable bed next to you and hold your hand as we try to fall asleep.

In March you have your final treatment for the clinical trial, but we already know it won't do anything.

It takes you multiple swallows to get anything down. You choke more often, mostly on water and your own saliva and phlegm. The suction machine that we all hate saves your life more than a few times.

In April, we all go for a ride in your beloved 1964 Ford Falcon. Last year you gave it away, to the man who helped you rebuild it all those years ago, a man you call "Dad." He's the father of your dearest soul friend from high school. She helps us take care of you and she is always there for you.

Just before sunset, your little sister lifts you from your wheelchair and gets into the front seat of the Falcon, then Dad drives us through the orange groves. From my position in back, as the golden sun floods the car, I can see you are smiling. The scent of sweet orange blossoms drifts in through the open windows and mingles with the smell of gasoline.

We file those beautiful moments away. Now it's a cold, cloudy day the following week, and the funeral director comes to our apartment. With this payment plan, he says, it'll all be paid for in a couple years. I'm circling the drain, you say. It won't be six months.

We start hospice. You agree only because this means you'll have ample meds for your stockpile.

Friends and family visit every weekend now. They come in to your room with loving smiles but behind their eyes they look stricken. You deflect, recount funny stories, ask them about their lives. You pose for pictures with them, make the shaka sign with your weakening hand limp on the pillow. Every time you say goodbye, you're sure it's the last time you'll see them.

I can't cry anymore, you tell us. It takes too much out of me. ALS is taking my ability to grieve.

It's Memorial Day, and you haven't had a bowel movement for five days. Heavy pain meds and dwindling food intake are slowing your digestive system to a crawl. You're in excruciating pain. I'm bumbling, I mess up and hurt you more. Our home health angel and hospice nurse take over, get you into bed and emptied out onto the chucks pads. You'll wear diapers from now on.

Except for one brief trip to the living room—the only time we'll use the Hoyer lift that's been lurking in the corner—you'll never get out of bed again.

We keep going, you say.

Even as your eyes take on a faraway look and we watch your body diminish, there's something different too. You're a little calmer, more at peace. You still tell hilarious stories and relive the good times.

You love when our home health angel comes, especially for an overnight when you two can talk and laugh all night, like you're at summer camp. She says *Shhh, we'll wake the girls*, but keeps giggling. Before she arrives, you have me draw goofy pictures on your diaper to surprise her, make her laugh.

July is here, and you're hardly eating. You speak less, sleep more, are not always there. But you still manage to make us laugh every day. You still look at me with love in your hazel-green ocean eyes, you still tell us you love us dozens of times a day. Thank you for today, you say every night.

July 11. Your normally high blood pressure suddenly drops to 80 over 60. Your sister and I look at each other over the nurse's head. We know what this means.

July 12. You try desperately to swallow water. It spills back out.

July 13. When we sit you up for the last time, you ask your sister to lift your arms, wind them around me. You kiss the top of my head, then we lay you back down and you don't speak again.

We surround your bed, tell stories, even smile and laugh at times. We've known this was coming for the last year, but it's still unreal, unthinkable. One by one, we tell you goodbye. It is a gift,to be able to say goodbye, though we won't understand this until later. We take turns holding your quiet hands and speaking our love into your beautiful eyes through endless tears.

It's July 14 at 3:38 p.m. and you're gone. Your forehead is smooth, the furrows gone. You are free. You didn't need your exit plan, you fought this bastard with everything you had, you clutched at life to be with us for as long as you could. You died a warrior on the blackest battlefield, wrapped in love. You didn't get two years. 🙢

JAY SMITH

The Cost of ALS Is Killing Us and Our Vets

I'M PART OF AN EXCLUSIVE CLUB WHERE I'VE DEVELOPED the most intimate, meaningful relationships of my life. Let's hope you never join. This club is where I met Matt Bellina, a thirty-year-old retired Navy pilot. He greets you with a genuine smile and handshake that immediately makes you want to be his friend. The kind of handshake your dad told you about when you were a kid. He's the kind of guy you could rely on for anything from parenting advice to bailing you out of jail in the middle of the night, no questions asked.

Matt lives with his wife and adorable toddler boys in picturesque Newtown, Pennsylvania. Yeah, his life is basically a Norman Rockwell painting. Well, except for one thing; he's in this club with me. The one where members share a common bond—we've all got ALS, an illness that has no treatment or cure and is one hundred percent fatal.

I first met Matt in the halls of the United States Senate last May, where we were trying to convince senators to help us get access to an experimental drug to treat our disease. Since that time, I've learned more about ALS from Matt than most doctors. He's done his homework. Military veterans are twice as likely to get ALS. Every year about six thousand people in the USA are diagnosed, and one thousand of them are vets. ALS is considered a "service-related" disease. No one can really explain this but the numbers don't lie.

ALS is a very expensive disease, costing each patient an estimated three hundred thousand dollars a year. The majority of patients bankrupt their families with the costs, and an even larger number simply can't afford the cost to stay alive, so they don't. Can you imagine? Having to stop *being alive* because it's too expensive to live?

Lucky for vets—well, kind of—the VA will cover your costs just like they would if you were shot in battle. In theory, at least. Matt explains, "The VA is obligated to take care of my medical needs. They pay up to a certain limit, so after that point you kind of have to make choices." Seems to make sense, right? You dedicate your life to serving your country, you get a terminal illness, you get care covered by the government. Unfortunately, it's not so black and white.

Matt describes his experience with the VA: "The medical staff is great, but unfortunately, they are beholden to layer upon layer of bureaucratic regulation. For example, from my diagnosis in April 2014, I was not seen by a VA physician until August 2015."

The average life expectancy for someone with ALS is eighteen months. We wouldn't leave a soldier with a battle wound sitting around waiting to see a doctor for sixteen months. Let me explain what can happen in those sixteen months. You can no longer walk, feed yourself, get dressed, or bathe. By the time you get into a VA doctor, it is likely you won't be alive. Matt goes on to explain, "I know of other vets in the same situation. I know a guy who is literally living in the VA hospital while he waits for approval."

In an ironic twist of events, Matt's local Home Depot recently discovered how long he had been waiting for the VA to get him a ramp so he could safely enter his own home and jumped in to help. In three days, they organized a group of volunteers and—with donated lumber from Home Depot—they built his much-needed ramp.

Getting back to our DC visit… we're at our last meeting with Alaskan Senator Lisa Murkowski, one of the few elected officials to make time to meet with us. During this meeting, Matt says something that makes the entire room go silent. Matt explains, "I honestly think nobody has looked at the costs. The Muscular Dystrophy Association estimates the total for all federal programs for ALS care is costing taxpayers $350-$450 million per year. You compare that to the $7.5 million spent on annual research and it really makes you wonder who is calling the shots and why they are still employed."

Yes, you read that right. Each year, we're going to spend $450 million to watch people die a slow, painful death, and are only willing to spend just *one percent* of that to try and save them. That's more than bad for our vets, it's bad for our country. It's embarrassing. Matt goes on to explain with all sincerity, "I am sad to say I will personally cost the taxpayer more than the total annual research budget when all is said and done. It is sad."

Sad indeed. Sad because hundreds of millions will be spent on care. Sad, because none of this care will make a dent in helping to save vets' lives. Sad, because another thousand vets a year will go through this with no end in sight. Sad, because membership to our exclusive club is so fleeting. On the bright side, with Matt's help, and your help, we *can* pressure our elected officials to make smarter investments, to direct more funds to research, and to take better care of our vets. And, maybe one day I can take a walk alongside my friend. &

JOSEPH BOLTON

Frankenstein Cliff: A Father's Love from Strength

I will guide you in the way of wisdom and I will lead you in upright paths. When you walk, your steps will not be hampered, and when you run, you will not stumble. –Proverbs

IN AUGUST OF 1969, IN THE DAYS LONG before cell phones and GPS, a young, athletic, twenty-nine-year-old man stood at the bottom of the trail to Frankenstein Cliff in Crawford Notch, New Hampshire. With him were two of his sons, ages five and four. The man had grown to love the White Mountains while an engineering student at Northeastern University in Boston and for many years, he would treasure black and white pictures of him and

his college buddies climbing Mount Washington.

The young father loved his boys and wanted to share the adventure of the mountains with them. The older one, named Joey after his father, was inquisitive and curious. Intuitive, he could grasp scientific and mathematical concepts that simultaneously astonished and intimidated adults around him. Joey, though, was forgetful, hated details, couldn't tie his shoes, and would struggle with the mundane. The same adults around him, at those times, found Joey exasperating.

The younger boy, Davy, nicknamed "Muggsy" by his father, loved to throw rocks. Muggsy also had an uncanny sense of direction in the woods. Naturally fearless, he always wanted to be the trailblazer on any expedition. His jet-black hair, ruddy cheeks, and dark eyes made him irresistible to the adults around him. Muggsy also tended to disappear on his own adventures, leaving a trail of broken windows (darn rocks), doors taken off hinges, and other expensive household disasters in his wake. It was safe to say that while Muggsy was irresistibly lovable, the adults around him would also find him exasperating, just like his brother. But the young father loved those boys, and that is why he now stood at the trail head of Frankenstein Cliff in August of 1969.

The father studied the roughly drawn map in front of him. Then, with Muggsy blazing the trail and Joey at his side asking questions, the father entered the woods. Passing under Frankenstein Trestle prompted questions from Joey: When will a train be coming? Will we be okay under the track? Will it smoke? Why do trains smoke? Muggsy looked around for a rock that would fit into his hand.

Leaving the trestle behind, the trail became steep and the boys scrambled up on all fours. A small rock would occasionally kick lose and tumble down the mountain. The boys should have felt scared, but didn't. Joey and Muggsy trusted their father and felt safe with him. The father's strength emanated from him, protecting the boys, and they always felt invincible within their father's love. As they continued to climb, the father would occasionally reach down and pull the boys up to the next ledge along the trail. Throughout his life, the father always had a soft spot for the underdog and would reach out to lift up the vulnerable around him.

At the summit, the little group stopped to rest and enjoy the view of the White Mountains and Crawford Notch stretching below them. Joey had to know the name of every mountain. He wanted to know if there was a trail up each mountain, which mountain was the highest, and how high it was. Muggsy found a nice rock, tossed it over the side of the cliff, and listened for the clatter below.

After a snack, the father led his boys further on the trail past the cliff. Did they miss the turn off loop to the bottom? Did the father overestimate the length of the trail ahead? No one knows, but hours later, the father and his boys would find themselves back on the road many miles north of the campground where they were staying. With cell phones still decades in the future, the father started the trek south along the road. Surely, someone would give them a ride back to the campground and the father would turn around and stick his thumb out with every passing car.

No one gave them a ride. Car after car would ride on by the father and his two very young sons. By this time, the boys were tired, and the father would alternate with one boy on his shoulders and the other by his side, hand in hand. The father never complained, or cursed the drivers, or felt bad for himself. In fact, for his whole life no one ever heard him say anything negative about anyone. But the father never forgot walking along that road with his boys, mile after mile, with no one giving them a ride. For the rest of his life, as long as he was able, the father would always give a ride to strangers thumbing it on the side of the road. Some of them were blind. One in New Hampshire was a philosophy graduate student. Another was a British man in his twenties touring the country with just a backpack and a deck of cards. Some were just people needing a ride. In any case, the father never passed anyone in need on the road like others had done to him.

It was many years later and the father awoke from an uneasy sleep by a chime beside his bed. His worried thoughts would never let him sleep as deeply or as long as he wanted to now. The chime rang again, and the father struggled to sit himself up on the side of the bed. He put his glasses on and looked at the clock: 1:22 AM. The father carefully swung his feet on to the floor and balanced himself.

He slept in the basement and his boy's room was on the second floor, so he readied himself for the climb up the two flights of stairs. Racked with the illnesses of old age, the man who climbed Mt. Washington years ago now struggled to walk across the room, much less two flights of stairs. But as he did many times over the last few months, the father ascended the stairs to the boy's door. Cracking the door open, he could see Muggsy's hair by the hall light. His hair was still thick and jet black for his forty-eight years. As the door widened, Muggsy's dark eyes came into view, just barely visible above his full CPAP mask. Relief shone in Muggsy's eyes as he recognized his father. Muggsy could not throw any rocks anymore, much less walk. He could barely move his finger to ring the chime to his father's room. ALS had taken everything from Muggsy, everything but love, and that love emanated from his father at the door.

Muggsy's requests for help came at all hours and quite often more than once a night. Tonight, the father lifted his boy and adjusted his position on the bed. It was tiring, but the father never complained, and he never failed to answer the chime. The old father loved his boy, and that is why he sat beside his bed and held his hand, in August of 2013.

Years passed, and Joey now stood alone at the foot of the Frankenstein Cliff trail. As he stood there trying to see the cliff from the parking lot, it suddenly occurred to him that he was now old enough to be his father's father when the three of them stood here fifty years ago. This thought quickly led to another: that he was the last person on this Earth who had any first-hand knowledge of what happened that day.

Muggsy died from ALS in November of 2013 and his father passed away in January 2019. The memory of that hike suddenly felt fragile. Trying to reclaim it, Joey took a few tentative steps into the forest and stood looking up the trail. He hoped that by standing on the trail and intersecting himself with this place of memory he would also intersect himself with that moment of time fifty years ago… and remember. Alas, no new memories would come. Nevertheless, Joey stood there, remembering his father's love. The father who loved them enough to drive three hours to the White Mountains to camp and take them on an adventure in the woods. Joey loved his father and honored him. And that is why he now stood at the trail head of Frankenstein Cliff, in August of 2019. 🐾

ABOUT MY BROTHER

David "Muggsy" Bolton was born in Pawtucket, Rhode Island on February 12, 1965, the second son in a family of five children with an older brother Joseph, younger brothers Peter and Patrick, and a younger sister Charlene. His parents were Joseph A. Bolton III and Carol A. Bolton (Savoie). After graduation from

Norwich University in 1988, Davy served as an officer with the 10th Mountain Division at Fort Drum and on deployment in Iraq as part of Operation Desert Storm. His last assignment in the Army was with the office of the Chief of Plans and Programs at the Pentagon. Davy's ALS was first noticed as a persistent pain and limp in his leg back in early 2010. By June of that year his diagnosis of ALS was confirmed. His resistance against the progression of his disease inspired those around him. When it became clear that he would be unable to overcome a severe blood infection, Davy made the decision to leave the hospital in order to die at home in his own bed. After one last look at his brother Patrick, Davy succumbed to his illness on November 10, 2013. He is mourned by his twin sons Michael and Andrew, and his siblings, numerous nephews and nieces, and friends. – JEB

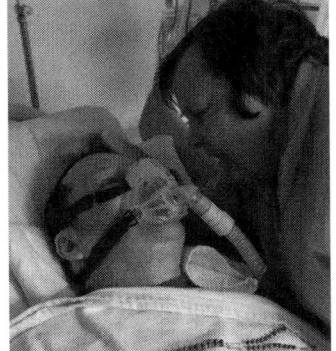

The photo on the facing page shows LTC Davy Bolton a year before the onset of ALS, meeting Dennis Miller. Above: Davy with brother Pete in March 2013, eight months before passing away from ALS. Right: Our mother tends to Davy a day after the miracle. This is the last photo taken of him while he was alive.

DANIEL CAMPBELL

ALS

I heard my father speak with a slight slur
I saw my father limping
I got the news that my father had ALS.
I saw my father with a cane
I saw my father with a feeding tube,
      because he couldn't eat or swallow.
I saw my father couldn't go upstairs
I saw my father use a walker
I saw my father in a wheelchair,
      because his legs could no longer function.
I saw my father in an electric wheelchair
I saw my father unable to stand without help
I saw my father unable to leave the house
I saw my father lose his ability to eat
I saw him lose his ability to speak
I finally saw that the monster that is ALS
      was finished destroying our life.
I saw the life leave his body
I see myself changed by the experience
I hope that no one else will experience it. ❧

DAVID O'NAN

The Nerves in Flames

I could think of myself
A dreamer in disguise
A burning oil, I feel no pain
I'm solid, I'm not a stepping stone
You put me in your unjust war, I survived
You tried to crush in my skull, you drank
You got away, I flew with angels for a few moments, survived
I've sinned against my family, I was too hard, too tough
To take a punch, I'd give the punch
The magic was my resistance
I lost and regained faith
I've been the loner, I've been the town jewel
Now what do you want to do to me?
A god or are you just a disease?
Prayer is my only creed, I just want to sleep
What is this burning, this twitching I feed
Why is my power ripping slowly from me
I can't stand, baby, I can barely breathe
My nerves are a jumping bean
You ask for bricks, a foundation
And all I can give up is my dream
This year is escaping me
Why do I feel that I'm losing touch with me
I try to cry, I've never felt that desire or need
What is this place, I can't escape it's claws deep inside of me

Is there an answer, please

My power just feels like sick, I can't walk

I'm stuck, all this laying I'm noodling quick

Where is my voice?

I have to tell them I love them

I see Jesus, see angels, see country outlaws in the clouds

My wife, I miss her, she is holding my hand

I can only feel the regrets of my years

My sons, my daughter are there to comfort me with memories

But I can only see the ceiling, and whisper that I love them

Why do I only see vapors?

Why the discoloring of my skin, brittleness of my bones?

The celebration of the holiday season

They will blame me for a ruin, my anxieties shut me down

My grandchildren are so confused

I find out that will never get to know me

Except through photographs and stories

Of the man that you knew

I'm not that man now, and want you to remember me

Like I was before the vultures feasted

Before another angel emerges from the vapors

And steps forward to pull me into the tunnels. ❧

MICHAEL THOMSON

Mooncake

In the heart of autumn
after the honeymoons,
candles in lanterns burn later,
our thoughts turn to
sweetness.

We will knead
with tenderness,
soft moons in our hands,
anticipating every delicate bite.

Let's meet and trade delights
when the path between our houses
turns silvery
and intimates our true desires.

Let me tell you about the lady in the moon. ❧

OSIEL MENDOZA

The Newest and the Youngest Generation of ALS

Adapted from a speech delivered at the ALS Therapy Development Institute's White Coat Affair in 2017

I WANT TO START BY SAYING A QUICK THANKS TO EVERYONE here at ALS TDI who have put on this event, and to all of the amazing people who work and fight just as much as we do to find a cure for this terrible disease. Thank you guys so much. You're amazing—every one of you.

I'd also like to thank Beth Hebron and everyone who is living with ALS who inspires me every single day to fight, and fight, and fight, and not to give up on this disease. You guys really deserve a round of applause.

I like to have fun, and I'd like to point out one special thing with me today that I actually use every single day—this cane here. I want to give a huge thank you to Corey Reich for handing it down to me. This cane is a very special thing to me. I use it every day, and it's made out of a bull's penis. So, being twenty-two and being in the same place Corey was nine years ago, I thought I might add some flair to walking around every day that makes me look a little bit better. So, thank you Corey. I really appreciate it.

I hope everyone's having an amazing night so far. I know I am. I wrote a very important speech that I'm going to get through. My name's Osiel Mendoza. I'm sure you guys are all wondering what kind of name Osiel is, because it *is* pretty weird.

I have a pretty funny story that I want to share with you all about a reaction that I once had to my name. About three years ago when I was at Oregon, I met the comedian Will Ferrell. I was his liaison at an Oregon football game so I was showing him around. I introduced myself and I said, "Hi, my name's Osiel." He responded by asking, "What the hell does that mean?" That will forever remain one of the best moments of my entire life.

My name is Osiel, and it's pronounced like the letters "O-C-L." That's a good way to remember it through a quick fun fact about my name. But who *am* I? I'm sure a lot of you guys are wondering who I am and why I'm standing up here talking to you tonight, and I want to take a little bit of time to tell you more about who I am.

I am twenty-two years old, and just about a year ago I was diagnosed with ALS. I'm from a small town in Martinez, California, which is just about a half hour from San Francisco. My obvious drink of choice is a Corona margarita. I just had a Corona before I came up here, so hopefully it helps me have a little bit more fun.

I'm recently married to my beautiful wife Bella who is here with me today. We have two beautiful kids—Jovie, a shih tzu, and Hendrix, a golden retriever. So, that's my life and I love my little family. I recently graduated from the University of Oregon—Go Ducks!—where I studied sports business and non-profit management. Over the four years that I was there I was working my ass off to gain as much outside work experience as possible. I was the Executive Director of a non-profit, I interned for the football team for three and a half years, I was Vice President of the biggest club on campus, and I worked for Peyton and Eli Manning's football camp in New Orleans. I was doing everything I could to set myself up for success so that I could find a job after college, provide for my family financially, and become a normal contributing member of society.

Heading into my senior year was a great time. I was getting ready to finish college—all the studying and long nights writing ten-page papers, all that good stuff. On top of that, I had just gotten a job at Dick's Sporting Goods that summer going into my senior year. That was all to save money for an engagement ring so that I could propose to my girlfriend at the time and love of my life, Bella.

Bella and I have been together since we were thirteen years old and in the eighth grade. At this time, I was getting ready to pop the question and make the big move. I'll quickly tell you how I did that. Last year, on October 19, we were celebrating our eight-year anniversary. Usually I get Bella a card, but for the first time in eight years, I didn't get her a card. That was bad on me, and it made her really upset. She was crying, and it was a tough day for me as well because, you know, I was being a bad boyfriend. I really screwed up.

But about two months prior to that I had bought an engagement ring and I didn't know what to do with it at the time. I didn't know how to ask her or when to ask her, so I was just hanging on to it. And, you know, right after I forgot to get her a card, I thought, "Well, this might be a great time to make up for it."

It was a big, beautiful diamond ring, and it was perfect timing. Two days later after that whole ordeal, I went to the store and bought her a card this time. The morning after, we went to the park and walked one of our dogs, Jovie. That's somewhere we went a lot. I brought her around to this private area in the park where it was really nice under the trees and shade. It was a beautiful day out in Oregon and I just knew it—I had the ring and the card in my pocket. It just felt like the perfect moment to do it. So, I pulled out the card and I gave it to her.

I said, "Hey, I'm really sorry that I didn't get you a card on our anniversary, but I hope I can make up for it with this."

So, I read all this romantic stuff—I feel like I'm a pretty romantic guy, and I wrote all this stuff in there. But at the bottom I wrote, "I'm sorry I didn't get you a card on our anniversary, but I hope I can make it up to you…"

And at the very, very bottom of the card I wrote: "Right now."

I gave it to her and she was reading it, and I was waiting for that cue where she would look at me and feel a bit surprised and excited… but it never really came, so she gave it back to me and said, "Thanks."

Now, my wife is an amazing person so I'm not bashing her at all, but she said "thanks" so I looked at her and asked, "Did you read the entire card?"

She said, "Well, I think so."

So I said, "Okay, well read it again, because I don't think you did."

She read it again and I was waiting for that moment again. At this point, I was going crazy. I didn't know if she was still pissed off or what was going on.

About thirty seconds later, I finally got the cue.

Her big, beautiful brown eyes looked straight into my eyes and I knew that it was time. I could feel the excitement and the love in that gaze, and that was my cue to get down on one knee and ask her to marry me.

Thankfully, after all that, she said yes. On October 22nd of 2016, Bella and I got engaged. It was the best moment of my entire life. But after experiencing that moment, I went through the worst time that I could ever imagine myself or anyone else having to go through.

On October 25th of 2016, just three days after I asked Bella to marry me and spend the rest of her life with me, I was diagnosed with ALS. I was told by a neurologist that, on average, I have two to five years until this disease takes over my body and kills me.

As a senior in college at the time, it was hard for me to accept this news. It took me quite a long time to tell anyone about it. I wanted to be a normal kid going into my senior year of college, and do fun things, and not have to worry about people treating me differently or acting differently around me.

But, Bella and I got married last month. It was an amazing time for us and our families. Bella, I think you deserve a big round of applause for everything.

I want to be a normal husband. When she needs a back rub, I want to be able to give her a back rub. And when she is craving ice cream, if and hopefully when she gets pregnant one day, I want to be able to drive to the store, on my own, and buy her a carton of chocolate ice cream if that's what she wants. I want to do whatever I can physically to make sure that she feels special, appreciated, and loved unconditionally.

We want to have kids *so badly*. I want to be a normal dad and teach my kids how to throw a baseball, or kick a soccer ball, and do the normal things that my parents did for me growing up. I want to be able to build them a tree house if that's what they want, and I want to be able to tell them that I love them with my own physical voice. But this disease is not going to allow me to do that without your help.

You have the power to help. I'm so extremely confident in everyone in this amazing organization, ALS TDI, and their fight every single day to make an impact—an effective therapy and a cure for this disease.

But, I'm not the only one. I'm not the only person that won't be able to walk, talk, or do things for their significant other, or watch their children grow up and graduate high school, go to college, and start their own families. There are others, and there are many of them. I'm standing here tonight representing all of them while I can still stand.

I'm the newest and I'm the youngest generation of ALS. And I really need to be the last. So please, please help. ❧

ADY BARKAN

I'm Dying—Here Is What I Refuse to Accept with Serenity

Written in 2018

ON SEPTEMBER 30, 2016, RACHAEL AND I CELEBRATED ONE YEAR of marriage and eleven years together by booking a hotel room in Los Angeles and going out for fancy Asian fusion. It was our first night away from our four-month-old son, Carl. Rachael had a great new job as an English professor in Santa Barbara. My career as a progressive activist was going gangbusters. We had just bought a beautiful house and could see decades of happiness stretching out ahead of us. We were the luckiest people we knew.

The next morning, we had brunch with my oldest friend, a first-year medical resident. I mentioned to her that my left hand was feeling weak, and after playing with it for a few minutes, she told me I needed to see a neurologist.

The following Friday, at the ripe old age of thirty-two, I was given my death sentence: The doctor told me I had ALS—amyotrophic lateral sclerosis—which would rapidly destroy all the connections between my brain and my muscles, leading to complete paralysis and death, likely in three to four years.

Three weeks later, our world was turned upside down a second time, when America elected a racist kleptocrat to the White House.

Like many people suddenly confronted with agonizing loss, I looked for answers in Buddhism. Pema Chödrön teaches us that when the ground disappears beneath your feet, the solution is not to flail around in a desperate attempt to find a handhold; it is to accept the law of gravity and find peace despite your velocity. Leave the mode of doing and enter the mode of being. Accept things as they are, rather than yearning for them to be otherwise.

Such radical acceptance is in tension with my identity as a movement builder. Activism is precisely about not accepting the tragedies of this world, but rather on insisting that we can reduce pain and prolong life. Social justice means creating a stable floor beneath our feet and then putting a safety net under that, to catch us if it suddenly vanishes: universal health insurance, affordable housing, unemployment benefits. Being part of a progressive political movement is about fighting back and building toward a better future. "Acceptance" is not part of our vocabulary.

The theologian Reinhold Niebuhr—whose most famous disciple, Dr. Martin Luther King Jr., would become the patron saint of American organizers—sought to resolve this tension in his Serenity Prayer: asking for the serenity to accept what cannot be changed, the courage to change what can be, and the wisdom to know the difference.

I have tried to internalize this worldview. I am no longer ruffled by quotidian nonsense, or even by the onset of new symptoms, such as when, earlier this month, I stopped being able to feed myself. I have come to accept that my ALS is progressing faster than average, that my body is wasting away quickly, and that what I have today will soon be gone. But there is one thing that still overwhelms me: when I imagine the future life of Rachael and Carl, who at the time of writing is now two years old. The weekend hikes, the afternoons on the basketball court, the evenings playing backgammon and doing homework, the mornings eating breakfast and laughing about the latest absurdity emanating from Washington, DC—these are the moments that I picture spending with them in an alternate universe. When this mental exercise brings me to tears, as it always does, I try to be at peace in my sorrow. But it is not easy.

Because of the weakness in my lips and tongue and my shortness of breath, becoming emotional makes it difficult for me to utter the words you are reading. My fingers have lost nearly all of their strength, so typing these words is impossible. Instead, I sit with my scribe, Aiyana, in my room. She now understands me better than anyone else, but even she has begun to ask me to repeat myself. Even when it is quiet. Even when we are sitting side by side.

For twenty years, since I was a freshman in high school, I have been writing newspaper op-eds and giving timed speeches—first on the debate team and at thespian festivals, later at press conferences and in community-organizing meetings. But never before have I felt so acutely the constraining force of my word-count limit. I know intuitively how many arguments I can fit into eight hundred words. I know when my three minutes are up, even without looking at my watch. But now, facing my final months of speech, the questions that I was taught to ask in high school have taken on new meaning: What do I want to say? To whom? And how?

I spent six weeks this summer driving across the country in a wheelchair-accessible RV with a dozen comrades in pursuit of answers, not only to my personal queries but also to our national ones. What kind of a country will Carl's generation inherit? And what will it take over these coming precious months to save our democracy? In twenty states and the District of Columbia, we met citizen-activists who are grappling with these very same questions, pouring their entire being into crafting tolerable answers. Some, like me, are dying and are throwing themselves into this November's elections because they know it may be their last chance. But many others with longer life expectancies are doing the same thing. It turns out that our collective time horizon is the same: We peer into the future and hope that our children's children will grow up in a more just and equitable society.

In nearly every congressional district, voters say that their top concern is health care. The high cost, the lack of access, the bureaucratic headaches—I heard these complaints in small towns, big cities, and suburbs from coast to coast. But these complaints are symptomatic of a much more profound problem: Our democracy is broken, and it seems that we have lost the ability to solve our collective challenges. Everywhere we went, we met voters who had been disabused of the notion that our elected representatives are pursuing the public good, disabused of the quaint idea that our government is of the people, by the people, and for the people.

And yet, throughout our travels, this cynicism was being overcome by a different emotion—hope. All around the country, we met people who can see beyond this dark moment into the bright light of another world. For the first time in many decades, our national politics are being shaped not only by fear and hatred, but also by our dreams for a better world. Each month, more organizers, activists, candidates, and elected officials are talking about reshaping American society in a radically humane way. This vision encompasses both negative and positive rights: freedom from unjust incarceration, racist policing, inhumane immigration enforcement, economic exploitation, sexual violence, and political disenfranchisement; and a set of public policies that gives us the freedom to thrive—debt-free education from pre-K through college, decent housing, the guarantee of a good job, clean energy, retirement security, and free and robust Medicare for all.

Focusing on the moment and immersing myself in the task at hand has been my salvation over the past two years. Peering into the future has been too dispiriting and too overwhelming. But there is so much to embrace in this very moment, so much work right here in front of us.

This was the message that I settled on somewhere between the cornfields of the Great Plains and the glistening waters of the Great Lakes: the notion that the cure to what ails American democracy is more American democracy; that our problems are created by people and that we can only solve them with people power; and that, as Rebecca Solnit teaches us, hope is not a lottery ticket that can deliver us out of despair, but a hammer for us to use in this national emergency—to break the glass, sound the alarm, and sprint into action.

What action? Voting is not nearly enough. This moment calls on us all to become organizers. To be heroes for our communities and future generations. To talk to our less political friends, neighbors, classmates, and co-workers, and to enlist them in this experiment we call American democracy. This is our Congress, our country, and our future for the making.

The past few weeks have borne witness to the potency of hopeful organizing. In the summer, the conventional wisdom in Washington held that Brett Kavanaugh was a sure bet to be confirmed to the Supreme Court. But in August, a handful of organizations began a campaign of civil disobedience to resist him, and in early September, as the Senate reconvened for what was supposed to be a smooth confirmation process, more than two hundred brave women said "no." They disrupted the hearings, focused the nation's attention on the moral stakes of the nomination, and created space for bold Democratic senators to push Kavanaugh on his immoral ideology and dishonest testimony.

Meanwhile, over 123,000 American citizens pooled their small contributions into a $3.5 million war chest and joined activists in Maine to deliver a clear message to Senator Susan Collins: If you vote for Kavanaugh, it will cost you your job. Collins, Fox News, and Senator Ted Cruz of Texas complained that we were engaging in bribery. That is their ideology in a nutshell: Corporate donors can buy all the access and influence they want, but regular American citizens must remain silent. This response is as old as class hierarchy itself, because there is no more dangerous threat to the status quo than collective action by the masses.

In late September, Kavanaugh's confirmation was thrown into doubt because Christine Blasey Ford testified that he had attempted to rape her in high school, and most Americans believed her. In an act of mass solidarity with Blasey Ford, thousands of survivors told their stories for the first time. The #MeToo movement has been building public consciousness for a year, and its legion of members were determined to prevent the Senate from repeating its embarrassing performance in 1991, when Anita Hill testified during the Clarence Thomas confirmation hearings. Hundreds of survivors and their allies boarded buses to DC; thousands more organized rallies and vigils in their hometowns. In Senate offices and elevators, on Facebook and around the dinner table, a mass movement of Americans insisted that we deserve so much more from our Supreme Court and our Congress.

Some of us even entertained the fantasy that we might be able to run out the clock until a new Congress convenes in January and possibly save this Supreme Court seat. One can hope. And then organize. And sometimes that struggle will pay off.

Sometimes, though, our struggle is not enough. ALS destroys my body, no matter how many medicines I take or exercises I do. Sometimes, oftentimes, white supremacy, violent misogyny, and rapacious capitalism rip apart our families and destroy lives, regardless of how well we organize. And sometimes, oftentimes, our stories are not powerful enough. Despite our best efforts, Brett Kavanaugh has been confirmed, and will do lasting damage to America and its people.

Yet it is in these moments of defeat that hopeful, collective struggle retains its greatest power. I can transcend my dying body by hitching my future to yours. We can transcend the darkness of this moment by joining the struggles of past and future freedom fighters. That is how, when we reach the end of our lives and look back on these heady moments, we will find peace in the knowledge that we did our best.

There is a seeming paradox embedded in the third part of Niebuhr's prayer, because the wisdom to know the difference between what we can and cannot change can only be earned through struggle. Neuroscientists seek a cure for ALS because they do not accept its inevitability. Organizers rage against the machines of capitalism with that same determination. It is only by refusing to accept the complacency of previous generations that the impossible becomes reality. For me, Niebuhr's prayer is most true if rearranged: Collective courage must come first, wisdom second, and serenity at the very end. ❧

ANGELINA FANOUS

Divine Intervention

IN 1968, A LIGHT IN THE SHAPE OF A WOMAN WAS SEEN radiating from the dome of the Church of Saint Mary in Zeitoun, Cairo. She disappeared after two or three minutes, but she reemerged the next week—again for just a few minutes. She continued to visit periodically, and crowds gathered, speculating that the light was the mother of God. The head of the Coptic Church at the time, Pope Kyrillos VI, investigated the sighting and concluded that it was, in fact, a Marian apparition. The (Muslim) president of Egypt, Gamal Abdel Nasser, reportedly built a bigger church across the street as a testament to his own belief that this was Mary. The Egyptian police and government searched for an earthly explanation, but no one could find a projector within miles capable of producing the image. The photos all look different from one another, as though the apparition were too ethereal to be captured in a single image. She continued to visit the church until 1971, almost three years after the original sighting.

In the early 90s I was a religious child, growing up Christian in Egypt, and my mother surprised me when she revealed that people still camped *en masse* outside Our Lady of Zeitoun during the Virgin Mary Feast, hoping to see Mary reappear. I was only five or six, but spending all night praying and reciting hymns squeezed between hundreds of people in the African summer heat sounded like, well, fun. Besides, what if she returned and we missed it? My family seemed foolishly unprepared, which meant I'd never get her *baraka*, or blessing.

We never went, and Mary never came back. But other miracles surrounded me. In the West, the word *miraculous* has penetrated our vernacular in such a way that it's become a synonym for *extraordinary*, while *extraordinary* has become a synonym for *amazing*, and *amazing* is just what you call the barista who remembers how you like your coffee. These words should mean something beyond our human capacity, but their place in our lexicon has shifted. None of these words would trigger thoughts of a supernatural force.

In Egypt, they do. There, miracles happen—and often. In Egypt, share a worry occupying your thoughts and people will spout off tales of the works of God. As a child, stories of icons weeping oil or the paralyzed suddenly walking fueled my belief that a divine hand often reached down to rearrange life's affairs. All you need is faith.

I lost my faith when I moved out of my parents' house after college. I didn't lose it in the sense that I was still looking for it—I lost it in the same way I had lost my childhood kitchen set when my family emigrated out of Egypt. I once imagined that a pale pink stovetop could cook eggs, but not anymore. I once believed that faith could move mountains, but not anymore. Still, on a sunny September morning last year, I found myself snuggled in the warmth and comfort of religion, faith, and wonderfully delusional hopefulness.

I needed to tell my parents that my twenty-nine-year-old brain was no longer properly communicating with my body—that it would, in no particular order, slowly stop telling my hands to move, then my arms, my legs, my jaw, vocal cords, and tongue. It would eventually forget to tell my lungs to expand, leaving me to slowly suffocate.

My parents were the last people I told, since I suspected that I'd tell them and then immediately have to begin planning their funerals. I didn't think my mother, who has a bad heart, has only one working kidney, and is a cancer survivor, could handle any more bad news on that list. My sister, Deedee, even suggested I leave out details about the course of the disease.

I flew from New York to Cleveland, where they live, with my backpack and an Arabic translation of the Wikipedia page on ALS. I was ten when we left Egypt, so I never learned which words meant "amyotrophic lateral sclerosis." I had only learned what the acronym signified in English a year prior, when I told a team of doctors that my left hand didn't seem to work quite like it used to.

When I arrived at their home, before I even had the chance to pull up the Wikipedia page or taste a bite from the spread of food my mom had prepared for my arrival, I was gasping for air, and my body was convulsing. I went into a delirious cry, the kind that made my eyes look like a cartoon character's and left the skin on my cheeks leathery.

"The doctors say the paralysis will spread throughout my entire body and I'll die," I managed to pronounce in shattered Arabic. I started to tremble, like my body does now when I'm upset or stressed or cold, rhythmically tossing back and forth in between my mother's arms.

"Don't say that!" she repeated several times. Her eyes were dry.

That entire week I stayed in my old bed from high school, asleep or not, only moving to occasionally use the bathroom. When I experienced a gust of energy, I relocated my laptop and my Netflix marathons to the couch. I'd occasionally answer texts from Deedee, in Washington, DC.

At night my mother slept next to me, underneath the old glow-in-the-dark stars from Spencer Gifts that are still stuck to the ceiling. She always woke up before I did and delivered a breakfast tray with her eyebrows raised, her eyelashes extended to her brow bone, and her jaw slightly dropped with a goofy smile, the same way she'd tell me I was no longer in trouble when I was a kid. While I moped, she went about her day, cooking and cleaning and occasionally calling out *ya rab* ("my God") in frustration. If even a single tear fell across her face that week, I didn't see it. She was tough, a rebel who scoffed at science. Regardless of what the doctors had said, God—she was certain—would have the final word.

"God has never embarrassed me," she said, her words spoken with a confidence that I badly wanted to share. But I wasn't sure that the same God who watches over suffering and injustice in the world would make my rather insignificant heartache a priority.

She told me to go to Egypt, convinced that I'd be healed there. This was my mom—God had never embarrassed her, and I definitely wouldn't, so by the end of the week I promised her that I would go to ask for a miracle. Eight weeks later I was on a flight to Cairo, numbing my anxious thoughts with tiny liquor bottles. For twelve hours I worried that a bishop, priest, or monk would expose that I lacked the one requirement to be miraculously healed—faith. I'd been taught to respect these people, that they weren't just people but servants of the Lord. That stuck with me, even as I shrugged off my religion. Before my trip, I had spoken to family members who seemed baffled and skeptical at how I, a young and otherwise healthy person, had suddenly become terminally ill. They all concluded, rather quickly, that "God tests us when we stray from Him." Even my cousin Evette, a pharmacist, told me, "He gives His toughest battles to His strongest soldiers. So put your faith in Him, before science."

Their judgment made me wonder what my tell was. What outed me as a nonbeliever? I had never told them about losing my faith. Had I spoken about my disease too matter-of-factly? Did I make a joke when I wasn't supposed to? It was apparent, whatever it was, and I doubted that I could mask it while I asked for a new central nervous system.

I traveled to Cairo with a purpose—to fulfill a promise to my mother—but I was also afraid that my skepticism flirted with mockery. I may have been going to be healed, but my instinct was still to approach the matter as a reporter, not a pilgrim. At first I couldn't even bring myself to tell anyone I was sick, and I spent as much time studying the occurrence of miracles in Egypt as I did looking for my own. In Egypt you don't have to look far: On my first day, I called a car to take me to Coptic Cairo, a small enclave of historic churches and religious sites, including one of the areas where the

Holy Family is said to have hid while fleeing Herod's death sentence. In the car, my driver, also a Christian, told me with zero instigation, "I witnessed a miracle this morning on my way to pick you up."

I hadn't told him why I was in Egypt, that I was sick, or even that I was a journalist. But it was Sunday and we were visiting ancient churches, so he led his small talk with miracles. He looked back in his rear-view mirror and occasionally flailed his right hand, showing off a coke nail in the process, as he detailed to me with both certainty and disbelief how only an hour earlier a priest had performed an exorcism and rid a young boy of demons.

"I don't believe in all that," I confessed. "Maybe the boy is just sick." But no matter how much I argued that people sometimes substitute a supernatural explanation for a scientific one, he wouldn't even consider it.

He dropped me off, and I was left to remember how ancient and beautiful and weird Coptic Cairo is. A stone wall three times my height surrounds the perimeter. Intertwined between the churches, which date back to the third century, are small square graveyards and limestone streets where people have been living since before the Arab conquest of Egypt. Walking up the steps to the Hanging Church, given its name because it's suspended over the Babylon Fortress, I passed couples and chatty teenagers and children with money in hand to purchase candles. Although it's technically the Saint Virgin Mary's Hanging Church, my eyes immediately focused on the icon and remains of Saint Demiana.

My parents say that when my mother was pregnant with my sister, the Virgin Mary came to my father in a dream and told him he would have a daughter. He would name her Demiana, and she would become a nun. A baby girl arrived. They named her Demiana. But she never quite made it to the convent. Deedee, as I have called her since we were little, is a glammed-up, sexed-up, vivacious version of me who loves strippers and gluten-free diets equally. She's eighteen months younger but treats me like the baby sister. In all fairness, she's now the more responsible one. Even though her eyes are wider, her cheekbones higher, and her lips poutier, she's the one who gets mad when someone says we don't look alike. She loves me so much that she broke her personal vow of exile from Egypt for the first time in fourteen years and decided to meet me for her Thanksgiving break.

That icon could've been what triggered my tears: Saint Demiana is legendary for her bravery. She was tortured on the orders of a pagan emperor after she refused to renounce her faith. Deedee is brave. She was the first family member I told about my diagnosis. I had tried to protect her, exhausting all possibilities, and I waited six weeks before I finally broke down and called her from outside the ALS Clinic at Columbia University Medical Center. She drove from DC to Brooklyn without even packing a toothbrush. That night we walked to dinner hand in hand, and we fantasized over margaritas and tacos about how I'd be the first woman to be cured of ALS. She promised she'd take care of me, and that my last days wouldn't be spent underneath those awful glow-in-the-dark stars in my old bedroom.

Within seconds of seeing the image of Demiana, my lips curled, my eyebrows puckered, and I wept at the entrance of the Hanging Church. It had been four months since I was diagnosed, and these bursts of uncontrollable tears had mostly subsided. When the news was still fresh, nothing specific provoked my tears—they just came again and again and again. I cried on sidewalks in Manhattan and Brooklyn. I cried on the subway platform and in the subway cars. I cried at my desk and throughout my office. I once cried in a bar, with a pink tequila cocktail in hand.

I even cried before the doctors confirmed my diagnosis. For almost a year, my neurologist seemed confident that as long as the weakness was isolated to my left hand, it was treatable. Then one night in April, walking down the subway stairs, I suddenly had to catch myself when my left leg started to shake and I lost balance.

That night I sobbed the entire way home, passing strangers who probably assumed a boy had brought on my tears. The weakness in my left leg meant I was out of options, but I lied to myself and said I was being dramatic. Two weeks later, on May 1, I turned twenty-nine, and as I blew out the candles on

Top: At the hanging church in Cairo, the author writes a prayer next to relics of saints. Bottom: The author places a paper with her name written on it next to the remains of Pope Kyrillos VI, the patriarch of the Coptic church from 1959 to 1971.

Top: *The water in this 2000-year-old well is linked to accounts of miraculous healing.*
Bottom: *Maximus Mahros, a volunteer at the well, fills a plastic bottle for the author.*

my birthday cake, I wished for anything but ALS.

On July 9, 2014, during my routine neurology appointment, I finally gathered the strength to tell the doctor about my shaky leg. I can still vividly see the expression in his eyes when he checked my reflexes and my feet bobbed up and down in midair. He took a few steps back and said, "It seems you're displaying upper motor neuron symptoms."

To most, that would probably sound like jargon, but I had read enough to comprehend that those words meant doom. "Are you talking about ALS?" I asked. He nodded.

When he couldn't get me to stop crying, he asked, "Tell me, what's going on in the Middle East these days?" Shocked, I stopped crying. "It's falling apart. Much like my body," I answered.

I left the office alone and confused. I chain-smoked, drank champagne, and spent the rest of the day annoyed at how inaccurately TV medical dramas depict the conversation I had just lived. The following six weeks I visited the best neurologists in the field, and when they thought I should repeat one test, I suggested we repeat them all. I just didn't want to call Deedee and inflict on her the worst possible news.

At the church I followed a lecture, wanting to learn about the history and powers of the place but unwilling to tell anyone my own story. One of the priests leading the talk spotted me and signaled for me to join the discussion. Although I had stopped crying, he maintained steady eye contact with me as he spoke. He was dressed in all black, with a long silver beard and big brown eyes. I wanted to run up to him, hug him, and list out the aches in my limbs and the pain in my heart, but I didn't. I sat and listened to him describe when the church was built, the details of the narthex, and how a painting of the Virgin Mary on the marble pillar was one of the unexplained things about the church. On one of the thirteen pillars in the church was a peaceful portrait of Mary with disproportionately large eyes and ears and a tiny mouth, in the common manner of Coptic art. But, the priest went on to say, no one knew how or when this particular icon had been rendered—because, he said, it was impossible to paint on marble.

"An angel could've painted it, or the Virgin herself, or a human," he explained. "There is no way to truly know."

"Well, that would be considered a miracle," said a forty-something woman, as if on cue.

The priest agreed and led his tour into another part of the church. I stayed behind and took photos of the miraculous painting of Mary, which was wrapped in clear plastic, as all the nice furniture at my great-aunt's house in Cairo had been when I was young. It may sound silly, but I believed him. I was taking photos with my iPhone, like some awestruck teenage fan, instead of Googling "Is painting on marble possible?"

After his speech I wanted to abandon my life in Brooklyn and go scrub floors at the church. Something in the story had made me feel insignificant and powerful at once, had made my pain seem relative. Who cares if I'm dying? Angels were painting.

I sat at a pew for a few minutes, still unable to ask anyone at the church for my own miracle, and then left to go drink from a 2,000-year-old well, inside a different Virgin Mary church in the patchwork of the area. The Holy Family is said to have hid in an underground room next to the well, and the miracle is supposed to be that it hasn't dried up in the intervening two millennia. As soon as I set foot in the church, I wept again.

I was pointed to a volunteer with crooked teeth named Maximus Mahros who manned the well at the church—he boasted about all the miracles he'd encountered in his time as a servant. A month before, he claimed, a terminally ill man had come to him to pray to the Virgin Mary and drink the salty water. When the man returned a week later, he told Mahros that he'd been healed. His doctors, Mahros said, deemed it a miraculous recovery.

"Would you like some water?" he offered, and I handed him a bottle to fill from the old paint bucket he lowered into the well. I chugged the water, and my face must have betrayed suspicion, because Mahros continued: "He called me today and said he'd come by next Sunday to show me his X-rays

Above: On March 12th in 1976, this Bible was found floating in the Nile outside this church, its pages open to Isaiah 19:25: "Blessed be Egypt, my people."

and blood work."

I asked for this mysterious man's number, but Mahros became evasive. He shifted his story, said that he didn't have it. He insisted that the man called him and never from the same number. I stopped myself before I asked about caller ID. "But he's coming next Sunday," he assured me. "You should come by and speak to him directly." I agreed and left.

I spent the following day touring churches and hearing about miracles that had supposedly been worked upon others, sobbing in each place from the minute I walked in. I went, as I had always wanted, to Zeitoun and sobbed. I sobbed as I collected oil for my wilting limbs. I even sobbed when I saw other people praying. I wrote pieces of paper with my name on them, and I sobbed as I placed them next to the icons and remains of saints. That would be the last time I recognized my handwriting. ALS would destroy my penmanship just a few weeks later.

Traveling through Cairo traffic and randomly crying at religious sites had wrung all the energy out of me. My right hand was also rapidly deteriorating around that time. Putting on socks went from a three-minute to a five-minute to a ten-minute chore. The Muslim Brotherhood had called for mass protests that Friday, and former president Mubarak's trial was scheduled for that Saturday. The entire country was on edge. Even the thick pollution that lazily idled over Cairo seemed anxious.

When Deedee arrived, eight days after I did, her presence helped palliate my grief. I took her to the well, where Mahros seemed surprised to see me, even though he was telling the same story he'd told me to other visitors. He said I was too early, because the man must have been attending Mass. I took him at his word. As Deedee and I went to have some coffee, she admitted that she believes in the supernatural and the possibility of miracles. I was happy, maybe even a little relieved, that she didn't hold my cynicism in her heart. Two unfiltered coffees later, Mahros was ignoring my phone calls, and it became evident that either the man wasn't coming or he didn't exist.

Deedee loved the idea of seeing her namesake's relics, so we walked to the

Hanging Church to light candles and continue my hunt for miracles. Saint Demiana's remains are locked in a glass case underneath the icon. They're concealed in a foot-long velvet tube that's embroidered with gold thread and smells like dried roses. Deedee squeezed my name into the glass case.

A few minutes later, I asked a tour guide to tell me the story behind the Virgin Mary on the marble, hoping to bask in the image of angels painting. Instead, he described a technique for painting on marble. He had no idea that his words were vacuuming all the magic out of the church for me.

He did tell me about a Coptic convent nearby to which a Muslim optometrist supposedly prescribed visits to suffering patients.

I asked for his name or number, a nonbeliever still doing my best to believe. After Mahros and the magical marble painting that wasn't magical at all, I was back to being the skeptical weirdo from New York.

He didn't even have the doctor's first name. He asked a few other people who were familiar with this phenomenon, but since no one verifies miracles and their faith is enough, nobody knew his name.

"You should go to the convent," one of them said. "The nuns would definitely know."

The Nativity Fast, when Coptic Christians give up all meat and dairy for the 40 days leading up to Christmas, had just begun, which meant the convent would be closed and the nuns would be praying. But something told me to chance it. When we got there, the iron gates were locked. Still unable to say why I'd really come, I told the guard that I was an American journalist reporting on miracles. He insisted that no visitors would be allowed in. I told him we wouldn't be long and asked whether the mother superior could make an exception. After a few minutes of silence, the iron gates opened and we entered into what felt like Eden.

I felt a strange sense of accomplishment that quickly vanished when I saw a young couple holding a baby in the middle of the convent. The bags under their eyes made it seem like they were deprived not only of sleep but of joy. Their baby looked too small to be out in the world, and they were clearly

Top: A visitor lights a candle. Bottom: Demiana Fanous places the author's name next to the relics of her namesake, Saint Demiana. All photos by David Degner.

visiting to bless their child and pray for their own miracle. The sight sent the grief I had so proudly overcome rushing back, but Deedee was right next to me, so I held my tears.

"I'm wondering if you could give me the name of the Muslim doctor who prescribes visits to this convent?" I asked, but before they spoke I knew the answer. They had never heard of the doctor or even the tale.

"Don't believe everything you read on the net," one of them said to me in a comforting, hushed tone.

"Well, I have a second inquiry," I said, finally able to form the question. "Is there someone who could pray for me?"

The same nun began to write down my name, and when she asked me what was wrong, the only words I could form through my sobs were, "The doctors can't do anything for me." I saw that I'd infected my sister with my tears. She walked over and held my hand. The nun asked whether we were sisters, and we nodded in unison. Deedee kept squeezing my palm to comfort me.

Maybe miracles, like anything else, are relative. In my early 20s I had agonized over carbs and boys, but now my thoughts only beg my body, "Please don't forget how to walk. Please don't forget how to walk. Please don't forget how to walk." Maybe my miracle is that my mother is living through her sadness—not by physical strength, love, or even a higher power, but by hope. Hope is what keeps us all alive, a beacon in a time of darkness. It's the most powerful force that I've ever encountered, and for some, nothing embodies hope more than prayer.

I waited for the nun to give me the speech about faith, about how I might have strayed from God, about how this "test" was only temporary. She didn't say any of that. "We don't live for this life," she told me. "We live for the afterlife. I wish I knew I would get to meet Jesus tomorrow."

Even though I'm young and agnostic and scared more of a wheelchair than of death, her words were more comforting than the promise of any miracle. ❧

DAVID O'NAN

The Courage Rhapsody

for my Dad and his battle with ALS

Silence… a cold breath mantra
Holidays voided by the entrapment of the body
Can't escape the seizing
The brittle bites my bones palpitate
Lost my nerves, and the winter took my shield,
My energy, my guiding hand, my memories I can only
Feel within my dream fog.
In my mind, I still have that.
I still have my love
Through all the night sweats,
Reminiscing when I was a stronger man.
A man with bravery,
Or the facade of… a man who could fight
Through the fires with the strength of tangled jungle wires.
I was easily scared, but nobody knew
Because it was safer to hide a heart of scars inside this chest,
I gave my soul to be caressed by the hope that is God's Word.
Now I am a man… not just your past,
But your future and in your cognizance.
Remember me as a man, a father, and your laughter and tears.
We will not struggle with the tugging of life's heavy rock.
We will lift it high, with our drums pounding, triumphant
Staring into black eyes. &

ABOUT MY FATHER

Peter Leon O'Nan was born on December 10, 1942. He passed away from ALS on Christmas night in 2016. He was one of six children growing up in Western Kentucky, working on farms and enjoying sports—he was a talented high school pitcher, and played on the basketball team. Despite his slim frame, he was very protective of his sisters and brothers. He was re-bellious and a slight loner at times, without a filter when he felt someone was wronging him. He joined the Air Force right out of high school, becoming an air policeman with postings in Texas, California, and the Philippines. He didn't fight in the Vietnam War, but had been willing to.

He was married once prior to my mother, and got divorced soon after getting home from the service. After marrying married my mom in 1969, they had three children together. My dad worked in many factory jobs, including in an aluminum plant which might have also contributed to his future medical problems. When I was two years old, my dad was on his way to work when a drunk driver going the wrong way hit him head-on. Dad lost consciousness and suffered head trauma, knee and leg injuries, and broken jaw. At one point as he was sent from hospital to hospital, he was wrongly pronounced dead. He survived but my family says he was not the same afterward. This would be the version of my dad I'd know—a man with a sarcastic sense of humor, who would watch University of Kentucky basketball with me, take me to see live wrestling matches, and ask for Long John Silvers for his birthday dinner. He always had time to listen to me talk when I said I needed to talk.

His falls began in 2014 while he was working for a recycling center. He had just had a stint a city magistrate for our small town of Sebree, Kentucky. We figured that his arthritis and bad knees from the wreck had gotten worse but by early 2016 he was falling all the time and it was clear something else was at play. It was a very scary moment when he fell off the porch and I had to attempt to revive his heart with chest compressions. I had no idea what I was doing, He pulled through but that was the beginning of the end. Through the year he went from hospital, to home care, to nursing home, to a VA clinic. By November he had lost his ability to speak. His once strong voice was now faint when he mustered the ability to softly say "I love you, son."

The night before he passed I played some of his favorite music to ease his mind: Waylon Jennings, Glen Campbell, Merle Haggard, amongst others. After I said goodbye and left the VA clinic on Christmas Eve, he soon fell asleep and never awoke. – DLO

EMMA WOLFE

The Day Before Valentine's Day

HE TEXTED ME YESTERDAY TO ASK IF I COULD DRIVE HIM TO the store to get Mom a Valentine's Day gift. It is a weird thing when you start to become a chauffeur for one of your parents. I told him I would, but only if he agreed to come with me to get my oil changed beforehand. It was a deal.

There are so many small pieces of our current reality with ALS that catch me off guard; like my instinct to reach for the volume dial on the way there, only to realize it's his wearied voice that my subconscious wants to turn up. Or all the odd looks you get when people see you buckling your Dad into the car.

Nonetheless, here I find us at the grocery store (along with twenty other husbands, boyfriends, and desperate men) in the card section, the day before Valentine's Day. I start to hold the cards up one by one as we read the cheesy generic lines, roll our eyes with disgust, and put them back. After about the seventh card, Dad just shakes his head and confesses that after so many years, they all start to sound the same. He asks me if I would lift his hand so he could scratch his nose. I start to lift his right arm. Grimace.

I forget that even though he can't use his arms, they're still open to pain. He says to lift his left; it doesn't hurt as much.

As my hope for finding the perfect sappy card begins to wane, he tells me to grab the card that says, *To the most beautiful woman in the world.* "That's the one," he says.

After a look at the back of the card, we begin scoffing, boohooing, and causing a vocal scene at its $7.99 price tag—all for words penned by someone who doesn't even know Mom on some glitter-drenched "sustainable" cardstock.

But it was the Day Before Valentine's Day, and here we were with all the other late chumps stuck in card inflation's trap. Right where they wanted us. So, with card in hand and the "your mom is priceless" speech given, we moved on to flowers.

Dad likes to meander. "What about this?" I pick it up. He shakes his head and moves to another section. "No, no, I think she would like this one," he says. I set the first choice down and claim the second. "Actually, I think I like the first one better." I return to choice number one.

We started at ten-dollar tulips, took some detours, and ended up with a $26 bouquet of yellow and pink roses and wildflowers. The perfect choice for mom.

"Oh wait. I was thinking we could also get some margarita mix," he says, which reminded me of my cheesy idea to get my husband some beer and put a sign on the front that says "Be(er) Mine."

Here I am: holding a bouquet of wildflowers, an eight-dollar card, some Jose Cuervo margarita mix, and a four pack of beer, laughing as Dad sarcastically offers to help while I juggle all of these things. All on the Day Before Valentine's Day.

We check out. I'm carrying it all. I ask him if he's getting tired.

"A little," he says.

We get to the car. I open the door and buckle my Dad into the passenger seat, lengthening the seat belt to reach across his body. Then, gently, I pick up his swollen, curled fingers and lift them over the belt.

So much of this strikes me as wrong, partly because it's not how things used to be, but more so because my core knows it's not how things are supposed to be. Despite all that seems wrong, there is one thing that seems resoundingly right: spending time with Dad at the store on the Day Before Valentine's Day. 🍂

ABOUT MY FATHER

David Brattain grew up in Greencastle, Indiana. After attending Greenbrier Military Academy and Lambeth College, he secured a position as a press technician for General Motors. He would go on to operate a successful dog kennel business along with his co-owner, his wife Jill. David loved anything adventurous including hiking around Mt. Rainier, four-wheeling, and snowmobiling. He loved dogs; his German Shepherd, Feuer, was his best buddy. Spiritual life was very important to him, and he was an avid learner and reader of anything related to the life of Jesus Christ. A true conversationalist, David loved talking to people and learning about their lives—he was often finding ways he could encourage or go out of his way to help others. He always had a smile, was never one to complain, and was a very gentle, humble, and incredible man. David was diagnosed with ALS in May of 2015 and passed away on January 26, 2019 leaving behind his wife, three adult children and their spouses, and two grandchildren. – EJW

RON SCHAFFER

This Thing

I often think of walking
Through fields of grass and streams
These things I took for granted
Now they're just a dream

Friends I used to have
Over time they drift away
It leaves me to assume
It must be seeing me this way

Our bodies have been ravaged
Minds are left to dream
Mornings we often wake up
With a silent scream

We all fight this battle
We know we cannot win
We know that we will never
Walk those fields again

We know we must keep fighting
Sometimes with just our brain
Our bodies may be broken
But the spirit still remains

Don't let this monster beat you
After all, it too will pass.
It's only temporary,
This thing called ALS.

Special

Why is it some are chosen
Singled out, it seems to me
Or is it some kind of honor
To have this rare disease?

It seems to skip the bad ones
It only takes the best
Must be we're special people
To be chosen over the rest

I don't know a single person
Who has this dreaded disease
That ever asked this question:
Why did this happen to me?

To the ones that went before us
Their memories must never fade
For all their pain and suffering
The sacrifices that they made

There has to be a reason
Although it's missed by me;

Are we just freaks of nature
To have this rare disease?

For Olly

Some men are meant for greatness
It's just meant to be
No man deserves more credit
Than a man we called Olly

He gave his time so freely
Helped so many in the past
Any problem you needed help with
You only had to ask

There's been many on this forum
But I have yet to see
Anyone that's done for others
More than this man we called Olly

So my friends we can't forget him
No one ever should
I'm proud to have known him
A man so filled with good

He's gone but not forgotten
As soon we all will be
Those left must always remember

This good man we called Olly
He always ended his posts
With the most beautiful repast
I always will remember it
Until the very last
Into the heart, an air that kills,
From yon far country blows.
What are those blue remembered hills,
What spires, what farms are those?

That is the land of lost content,
I see it shining plain;
The happy highways where I went
And cannot come again. ❧

MICHAEL THOMSON

The Train

MY OLD MAN AND I GOT INTO IT AGAIN AFTER HE FOUND the whiskey under my bed. It was nothing new. My run-ins with him had begun about three years ago, when he caught me smoking with Holly, the girl who lived next door. He made me smoke the rest of the pack in front of him, one cigarette after another, until I threw up. It was supposed to teach me to hate smoking, but all I learned was not to smoke eighteen cigarettes in a row. Then there was the time he caught me with one of his *Playboys*. He whipped me with that old brown leather belt of his—the one I'd made for him at Father Hitchens' summer camp. I had tried jumping to get out of the way, but even after ten beers he still managed to catch me on my thirteen-year-old legs, and I had to wear shorts for a week after that because it stung when my pants rubbed up against my knees. But this time, this time he got really angry. This time when he went for his belt, I showed him my fists. That was all it took. That old bastard really knew how to throw a punch. Though he only hit me once, he made sure it was a good one.

"You know damn well it's a sin to steal!" he growled, as his beer-filled fist landed flush, fattening my lip. When I came to, he was gone. I got up off the ground, went straight to my room and closed the door. In the morning, I heard him grumbling to my mother about how disappointed he was in me, that I hadn't taken the summer job he'd set up for me down at his factory. I just lay there, still angry, pressing on my lip. I wanted to make sure it stayed good and swollen for my mother to see. She didn't bother to say anything about it, like it didn't even happen.

I spent the next day hanging out and smoking with Holly in the field behind our houses. We were still friends after the cigarette incident. She had rosy cheeks and supple knees, and I'd been trying to get with her all summer. We just lay in the grass talking for hours, mostly about what it'd be like to one day be on our own. Problem was, she had great parents. And although she was always there to listen to me, I knew she really didn't understand how much I wanted to just get up and leave town.

Later in the evening, we heard my old man's rusty old pickup pull into the driveway.

"You'd better go," she told me.

"You're right, I better."

I leaned in to kiss her, and she gave me her cheek. I couldn't blame her; I'd been at my lip all day.

I went in through the side door of the house, knowing he had to walk by me on his way to the kitchen. When we approached each other in the hall, he didn't even look at my lip. His eyes stayed fixed on mine, watching me, almost daring me to do something.

On the other side of the house, I heard his after-work ritual: straight to the fridge, a beer-crack, straight to the chair, the familiar remote-click, then the television crackling as the evening news came on. In the kitchen, the dinner table was being set. When the first commercial break came on, he got up and went back to the fridge for another beer. When he did, I went upstairs and locked my door. I scribbled a note, grabbed my phone, my wallet, and a couple candy bars for dinner, and I climbed out my window. Down the tree I went. I was certain that by the time they read my note, I would be clear across Santa Fe.

After a couple hitchhikes and an hour of walking, I made it out to the highway. Then I saw it: the train. It was long and clackety, a grain and cattle train. I didn't know where it was heading, but I knew for sure I wanted on it.

The train was going slow enough for me to run alongside and throw myself onto it. And since it was my first time ever to jump a train, I hopped onto the first rail-car I saw. Once I managed to pull myself onto the train, I walked around the inside of the car and kicked some hay into a pile to lie on. Then the train picked up speed. I passed the time away by counting the cows that went by outside the door. I got up to about eighty-nine before the clicking of the wheels on the track made me drowsy. Just as I was about to nod off, my phone rang. I looked at the display. It read Mom. Instead of answering it, I turned my phone off and went back to listening to the rhythmic clicking of the wheels until I fell asleep.

On the second day, we climbed through what I figured were the Rockies. The train slowed to a crawl and at one point I got off. I walked toward the rear of the train and jumped into the next open door I saw. Pleased, I'd found a relatively cleaner car, one with a little less odor. I unwrapped my second candy bar and ate half of it, bit by melted bit, saving the other half for later. After I put it back in my pocket, I turned my phone on and listened to the messages from my mother. In all there were five. She was pleading for me to call, to come home. I heard the worry in her voice and I almost wanted to call just to let her know I was okay, but she handed the phone to my old man so that I could hear him pitch a half-baked request for me to come home too, so that we could "figure it out." Then he handed the phone back to my mother. Right before she hung up, I heard him in the background, "Ah, leave 'em be. He'll learn the hard way!" His voice angered my fists into a tight clench and then with a *fuck you* I threw my phone out into the Rocky Mountain wilderness. I never heard it land, just the click-clacking of the tracks beneath me. I stood there at the door for a long while, regretting having thrown it. I sat down on the floor again and stared at the hills going by, recalling all the fights I'd had with him. The regret about throwing my phone soon passed.

I just lay there listening to the train until it got dark. We weren't near any towns, so it got dark as pitch, fast, and every once in a while, we passed a red light. I figured the lights were for marking distance along the track, but they always came as a surprise, the sudden flash of red filling the car. It always made me jump. I must have fallen asleep somewhere between the twelfth and thirteenth red light.

When I woke on the third day, I learned just how far the train had taken me from Santa Fe. The last sign I saw read Hell Creek, Montana. My empty stomach tightened even more. I removed what was left of the second candy bar from my pocket and finished it with one swallow. It wasn't enough, though. I was still hungry. When the train slowed to a crawl again, I hopped off. For all I knew the train wasn't going to slow down again for a long time, and I had just eaten the last of my candy bar. I was also very thirsty.

The suddenness of the ground stung my ankles. It felt great; I felt alive. I was doing what I'd often dreamed of, going out in the wilderness, a man, big and free, completely under my own power. I looked around. It was an incredibly flat plain in every direction. It appeared to go on forever. I'd never seen so much sky in comparison to land. But with the sun directly overhead, and the sky so blue and unadulterated by clouds, how big I'd felt quickly faded. It occurred to me that I hadn't seen or spoken a word to anyone in three days. I brushed the thoughts of home from my mind and set off on foot.

Far off in the distance I noticed a white pickup truck speeding across the horizon, kicking up a long trail of dust as it went. It was moving along at a fast clip, and from my estimation, it appeared to be about a mile away, maybe two, across hard-packed soil and scattered brush and rocks. I set out toward it, keeping my eyes on the trail of dust, but with each step the dust thinned lighter and lighter, and before long the truck was gone and the dust had all but settled back on the road.

After a good while of walking, I turned back to look for the train tracks, thinking it would give me an idea of how far I'd walked, or if I was even walking in the right direction, but I didn't see anything resembling tracks.

All I saw was wide-open land. When I looked back to where the road should be, it too had disappeared, blended back into the landscape. I spun around several times, alternating looks in front of and behind me, and lost track of which direction I had first been heading. I checked the sun. It was still directly overhead. I decided on a direction and walked toward where I believed the dirt road was. I walked for another five minutes and then I heard it: a distinct rattling directly below me. I'd never heard one before, but being out in the open range, I knew in an instant that I was stepping over a rattlesnake. I leapt away from the rattling sound and began to run, but before I was able to get clear of it, the snake had already sunk its fangs in me. When the poor animal tried to release its bite, it was unable to. Its fangs had gotten caught in the fabric of my trousers. Too afraid to stop, I kept running, and all the while the snake was hissing and swinging around my legs, trying to trip me. Then I did something I'd never dream I could. I reached down and grabbed the snake by its tail, and with one adrenaline-fueled tug, I ripped it free of my jeans and let out a howl as I slung it into the air, as far away as I could. The snake continued to hiss and rattle as it flew. The damned creature was just as afraid as I was. Then I heard it land with a thud and go quiet. I looked down at the bite and saw four puncture wounds. There was blood, a lot of it. I knew I was in trouble. I recalled being told by someone on a camping trip once that a good thing to do was to try to suck the venom out, but I couldn't reach the side of my thigh with my mouth. Then I realized it was my old man who had told me.

Remain calm, I thought. What would the old man do? Running to the road was all I could think of, but where was it? I decided the most important thing to do was to tourniquet my leg, so I sat myself on the ground, fastened my belt around my thigh as high up as I could, and that was when I felt a light-headedness coming over me. I fastened the belt a notch tighter, but it didn't help. *This can't be happening*, I thought.

Soon, I didn't even feel the bite anymore. My leg had become heavy, numb from the venom. When it started to spasm, I stood up, thinking I could just walk it off, or make it stop. I prayed that I would come across the road, where someone would see me and pick me up. I needed to get to a hospital, or somewhere that had some anti-venom. It was my only hope. I vowed that if I lived, I'd go straight home, quit the smoking, and start walking more of the line my old man wanted me to, maybe even take that job he'd offered me at the factory. I just wanted my life back.

I walked for another seven minutes or so, until my breathing labored. I knew the venom had made its way to my heart. I began seeing flashes of orange and white, and my ears started to ring. I heard the echoes of hawks in the air as the heat of the sun bore its weight down on me. After a few more paces, I collapsed on the ground. I lay there, looking up. I felt myself sandwiched between heaven and hell, between the heat of the ground and the pulsing sun above me. While the venom coursed a fiery trail through my veins, I stared back at the sun watching me, and off in the distance I heard a train's whistle cry. 🙢

ERIC VALOR

My Strings Sing for Renaissance

The strings
To my Meat Marionette
Have been cut!
And so we
Round up the usual suspects.
As they are released
One by one
I realize that
Lying around in bed all day
Isn't as decadent as it sounds.

The floppy foot
Made a Goofy step
As it marched up the leg.
After the
Fall Season
I decided to have a seat.
Then I
Let my fingers do the walking
Until they took a hike.
I can't even
Give myself a hand.
And the creeping uneasiness

Took my breath away.

Unlike Mick
Time is not on my side
Although I seem to have more
Than ever before.
Now cyborg is as cyborg does
And I wait for
The bright near future
Where once again
Gravity is my friend.

Locked-In Blues

Ever since you left me
I'm unable to move
Frozen and flaccid
I got the locked in blues

I lie in bed
No connection to my head
Wishing I could be
Somewhere else instead

My tired eyes
Are compromised
My hands are tied
My legs petrified

Don't want to be here anymore
But I'm too afraid to
Go back home

I got the locked in the locked in blues
I got the locked in the locked in blues
I got the locked in the locked in blues . . .

You took my breath away
My identity too
You took it all
I got the locked in blues

I can't eat
I barely sleep
I just sit
And silently weep

My tired eyes
Are compromised
My hands are tied
My legs petrified

Don't want to be here anymore
But I'm too afraid to
Go back home

I got the locked in the locked in blues
I got the locked in the locked in blues
I got the locked in the locked in blues . . .

Just a prisoner of myself
Just a prisoner of myself
Just a pitiful prisoner of myself

Iki & Etta

for Squar, in thanks

They call to me;
Rotund
Party-colored bodies
Beckoning in rhythmic promise.

Caress our heads,
They whisper:
Let us tell tales
Of instinct and passion.

Tactile touch
Brings sonic sense
Which hypnotizes
And keeps transfixed.

Hand to skin
We pat
And pound
And slap
And roll.

Hold my heartbeat
And guide its pulse.

Let me find the tempo
To which my soul can dance.

Direct my dreams
And transform my temper.

Teach me about my nature
And reach my song inside.

Be the voice
By which my spirit speaks. ❧

JAY SMITH

Man with ALS Wants To Be Turned Into a Robot

IN 2014, A THIRTY-SIX-YEAR-OLD AUSTIN, TEXAS MAN WAS given less than two years to live. He was diagnosed with Amyotrophic Lateral Sclerosis, commonly referred to as Lou Gehrig's Disease. Now confined to a wheelchair, unable to walk, eat, use his arms, or speak, he is making a public plea to be turned into a robot. I decided to visit Jay Smith in the Austin home he shares with his wife, two young daughters, and slightly annoying chihuahua to understand more about his bizarre public request.

Smith—who speaks through a computer—used his eyes to type his predicament: "Even though I can no longer command my muscles to move any part of my body, I am otherwise very healthy. My mind is sharper than ever. It seems like such a waste to die." Smith is hoping his public plea will reach the right scientists who specialize in robotics.

I ask Smith where he got this idea and his eyebrows raise with excitement

as he types his response. "*RoboCop* came out like thirty years ago so they [the scientific community] obviously know how to do it," he exclaims as he feverishly types with his eyes. "I don't understand why no one else has been turned into one?" Smith, who seems of very sound mind, appears to have quick wit and deep intelligence, and who was recently forced to retire as CEO of the music tech company Livid Instruments, is strangely oblivious to the difference between technology in movies and in real life.

We move into his kitchen so his eight-year-old daughter can feed him through a tube that connects through his abdomen. He explains why he now wants to become mostly robot: "It's been seventy-five years since Lou Gehrig died and there is still no treatment. Even with the massive influx of cash from the Ice Bucket Challenge in 2014 the ALS Association can't figure out what to do and is still sitting on most of it. We've pleaded with the FDA to change the outdated rules for testing experimental drugs but they really don't care about rare diseases. Obviously, the medical community isn't in a rush to cure it, so I figure what the heck."

Smith, who is already surrounded by technology he has made himself to control things in his environment with his eyes, describes what he would do with his robotic body. "Mostly boring stuff like gardening, helping my kids with their homework, and driving them to soccer practice, but if part of the deal was I had to fight crime or do appearances at kids' birthday parties and stuff, that would be totally fine with me."

Smith shares with me that he has been trying to get a hold of Hollywood engineers before it's too late. "My daughter starts first grade next year and I'm shooting to be alive so I can see her walk her into school on the first day. I'm hoping a Doc Brown type will hear about my story and be able to help me out. Ideally, I'd like to keep most of my body and augment it with robotics, but I know beggars can't be choosers, so I'd settle for a C3PO type deal. I just want to look somewhat human. After a long pause, his eyes fill with tears and he turns to his wife who is the only one who understands his very slurred speech and says, "I just want to live to see our girls get married. If medicine can't help us, maybe technology can."

Smith says anyone who wants to take on his challenge can reach him through his Facebook page. Others who want to help but can't turn him into a robot can sign his change.org petition to urge the FDA to allow him access to experimental treatments. ❧

DISCLAIMER

This is a satirical story written by the author, about the author, to illustrate the reality of living with an untreatable disease in the year 2016. I am fully aware that *RoboCop* isn't real. However, I would not turn down the chance if it presents itself. – JS

RICHARD BEDLACK

How ALS Left Its Mark on Me

IN THE PAST EIGHTEEN YEARS, I HAVE SEEN MORE THAN TWO thousand patients with ALS. They have all touched me in some way. This is the story of one that left a special mark on me.

ALS stands for amyotrophic lateral sclerosis. Better known as Lou Gehrig's, it is an incurable degenerative motor neuron disease. Patients affected by it lose the ability to walk, write, dress, speak, swallow, and eventually breathe. Death or mechanical ventilation occurs on average three years after symptom onset. For me as a doctor it has always been terrifying to watch. It has made me feel powerless. Textbooks say there is little to offer against this disease, and that no one ever beats it. Thankfully textbooks can sometimes be wrong.

I started my career trying to fight ALS through science and technology. I read every paper I could get my hands on and travelled the country talking to experts. I used what I learned to build a specialized multi-disciplinary ALS clinic here. My team got very good at measuring the disease in various body parts and knowing when to recommend things like feeding tubes and ventilators. I relished small victories like drying secretions, slowing weight loss or reducing carbon dioxide levels. I thought this was the best I could do. Then I met Tim.

At age twenty-nine Tim was one of the youngest people I had seen in my ALS clinic. He and the many friends that accompanied him looked even younger with their spiked and colored hair, piercings, and many tattoos. As we went through his history and exam, which were unfortunately classic for familial ALS, I noticed that Tim and all his friends had one tattoo they all shared in common: a black swallow. In fact, Tim himself had an entire sleeve of these. I asked about them.

Tim told me about his mother, whom he hardly knew. She died from ALS when he was very young. She left him a book, and on every page of this she had drawn a swallow. When Tim turned 16, he had every one of these copied onto his arm. When it became clear that Tim was also developing ALS, many who loved him got at least one of these to show their solidarity. They called themselves the Often Awesome Army.

Tim's body got weaker, but with the help of his Army his spirit stayed strong. They came to clinic as a unit, smiles on their faces, great stories to tell, and lists of the latest ALS research they wanted to discuss. They helped Tim participate in some of these studies, including one that required him to travel back and forth from Miami. When he needed help at home, they took shifts. When he needed expensive equipment such as an eye gaze system for communicating, they held fun events like concerts and tattoo-a-thons to raise money. Instead of lamenting or hiding Tim's losses, the Army created a series of YouTube videos about them. These were superbly crafted and well balanced, winning numerous awards including the Webby People's Choice Award. Through these, half a million of us laughed and cried as we watched Tim and his Army take on various challenges together including his wedding night with what was by then near total paralysis.

Inspired by the power of this group's approach, by the way they made ALS less intimidating, I started thinking about getting my own swallow tattoo.

I did some research to be sure this symbol did not have any unexpected meaning that might get me in trouble. I learned that the swallow is an old tattoo that sailors used to get because it is the first bird they saw when land was approaching. For them it meant they weren't lost at sea... that home was near.

The day I got my swallow, Tim was hospitalized with respiratory failure and had to be put on a ventilator. I travelled to Greensboro to see him. He got a big kick out of my new tattoo... he thought it was too small, that it looked like a freckle. He laughed when he heard that I had asked the tattoo artist to describe their sterilization techniques and that I wanted written post-procedure instructions. He guessed that it took longer to answer all those questions than it did to draw the tiny tattoo. He was right. He asked for an update on stem cell research. That was the last time I saw him.

Tim died in his own home, surrounded by his Often Awesome Army at age thirty-one. At the time of his death the muscles in his face, arms, and legs were completely gone. His heart was as strong as ever.

I am left-handed and my swallow is on my left wrist. Each time I sign a chart, my tattoo pops out of my sleeve. It reminds me that I have more powerful weapons to offer against ALS than medications and equipment; I am now always careful say something funny, optimistic, or hopeful to my patients. It reminds me that some people can use these to beat ALS by holding onto who they are in spite of the disease. It reminds me of Tim. &

JOSEPH BOLTON

ALS and a Rosary Miracle

ONCE IN A WHILE, WHEN GOD LOOKS DOWN ON US WITH love, He drops a soul into the world like a pebble gently tossed into a pond. Like a pebble, the soul makes waves that spread throughout the world before it all too quickly slips from our sight. My brother Davy was just such a soul.

I could talk at length about Davy's quiet generosity, his love for his family, for his sons Michael and Andrew. I could also write about how since childhood Davy was a natural leader and how even at a young age the neighborhood children would follow him around. As an Army officer, Davy's men loved and trusted him. No, my limited time and lack of eloquence cannot do justice to almost fifty years of a life well-lived.

I do want to take a moment to share with you how Davy inspired us during the last couple of years as his struggle with ALS progressed. Jesus never promised us an easy life when he said that we must pick up our cross and follow Him. It is a paradox of our faith that whom Jesus especially loves, he gives a great cross. Davy was Jesus's pebble tossed into our lives and the waves made through Davy will continue to radiate throughout our world for many years to come.

Davy's illness inspired compassion, love, and generosity in others. Davy's suffering became an opportunity for people to think of others instead of themselves. Neighbors, friends, or even strangers would commit acts of love in Davy's name. People would come over to help around the house, bring or cook food, and bring comfort to Davy, my parents, and Davy's boys. Jesus told us that whatever you do to the least of my brothers you do unto me. Therefore, every act of love and kindness directed to Davy and our family was also an act of love toward Jesus Himself. Davy's illness inspired compassion in others and through it, Jesus brought His love to us while we, in turn, became more loving people to our neighbors.

Davy's illness also inspired a spiritual awaking in those around him. One of Davy's fellow Army officers spoke to me about how Davy's inner beauty brought her back to a deeper love of her Catholic faith that she had lost. Others began to pray—some for the first time. Some of us began to pray the Rosary daily. Others started to attend daily Mass. At first, these prayers were for Davy and our family, but as time went by, Jesus used our newly inspired prayer lives to draw us into a deeper, loving relationship with Him.

A week before Davy passed away, he was hospitalized for three simultaneous blood infections. What happened to us in the hospital during that stay provided the most profound and mysterious lesson. While my brothers Peter and Patrick, our mother, and I sat with Davy, his blood pressure took a sudden, drastic drop. Davy became unresponsive. His doctor ran through all the checks, poking and pinching Davy, even yelling in his ear. Nothing. Even a light shined in Davy's eyes brought no pupil response. Although Davy still had a weak pulse and low blood pressure, he was, for all practical considerations, dead.

In effect, Jesus was using Davy to bring us into a closer bond with Him.

At the time, the medical staff had no options to revive Davy. It was everyone's belief that this was it: clinical death was imminent. A few moments later, by sheer coincidence, Davy's parish priest arrived. We all gathered around

Davy and began to pray and talk to him. We stood and prayed out loud there for two hours to include two full rosaries, the Divine Mercy Chaplet, and the Daily Office. Slowly and miraculously, with no medical intervention, Davy began to come around, opening and closing his eyes, and mouthing some of the prayers with us. Later, Davy eventually came around long enough to see our sister Charlene and cousin Jim for the last time. He also shared some final moments with Michael, Andrew, and our parents.

For those of us who were there, this was a profoundly moving experience that we will never forget. As I reflect on what happened, three truths become apparent:

We didn't pray alone. The Guardian Angels of everyone in that hospital room were praying with us.

Prayer isn't about repetition, incantation, or even changing God's mind. Prayer is about opening ourselves to the love and generosity of God.

Lastly, no one lives without prayer. Prayer is life itself, and even when we don't pray for ourselves, others pray for us and sustain us. It could be our parents and friends who pray for us. At the very least, our Guardian Angels pray for us constantly even if we don't believe and pray. Like the air around us, prayer is life. We don't appreciate what it would mean to live without prayer until it's gone.

In his epistles, Saint Paul wrote that we have a cloud of witnesses watching over us and cheering us on from above. Davy is now among them. From there, he will continue to pray for us and be a part of our family. Like the pebble dropped into a still pond, Davy has now slipped past our sight, but the waves he made still radiate outward. We must continue to be those waves and to go forth and inspire others as Davy inspired my family, with acts of love for our neighbors and with unceasing prayer for others. ❧

KYLE CONNORS

Reflections

2017

MAY 2: It is ALS Awareness Month. So, what can people learn about ALS? Most people are all too aware that it's a nightmare of a disease with no proven treatment. Most know that once diagnosed, PALS face a two-to-five-year battle before succumbing to this disease. Most people already know that while PALS' muscles gradually die, their minds remain intact in a twisted way so you can witness the toll the disease takes on your loved ones.

How can I help with spreading awareness this month? Each day this month, I'm going to try to share something I miss from my life that ALS has stolen from me. I'm not doing this from a bitter perspective. I've accepted and continue to accept the changes and challenges presented to me by this journey. Now you're probably thinking: Kyle, this sounds depressing as hell. I'm just going hide you from my newsfeed. Two things: I will keep it light, and it's better than another political post, right? I hope this will not only give you guys some insight into who I am but also into how ALS can affect even the simplest tasks.

I think the biggest thing I miss is being able to hold and hug my kids.

I would love to be able to squat down, take Em and Brycie in my arms, stand up, and squeeze them until they made me stop. The other night, while watching a movie, Emma fell asleep in my room and I would have given anything to have been able to pick her up, carry her upstairs, and tuck her into her bed for the night. Bryce literally gives the best hugs, and I just wish I could hug her back.

MAY 10: Most days I miss being able to walk upstairs because I'd love to tuck Emma and Bryce into bed one more time. Today I wish I could just reset my freaking router.

MAY 11: I miss not having to worry about being able to get into my car. And yes, while there was a time after Bryce was born when I put on some weight (some being a lot), and I might have had a tough time squeezing into my car if the person next to me parked too close, it was never a concern. Being in my power chair full time requires the use of a van to get around. Now most decent people understand that the areas of a parking lot with the diagonal stripes are not actually parking spots. So, as you can probably imagine, I was slightly perturbed when I got back to my van after my trip to the ALS clinic on Tuesday to find some moron parked right next to me.

Fortunately, the attendant was nice enough to help direct traffic and I was able to get into the van. He also assured me that he would write a ticket for the car.

MAY 14: While I've been sharing things that I miss that ALS has taken from me, there's still a lot that I have that I'm incredibly lucky to still have. I am so lucky to have the amazing Mary Connors for a mom and caregiver. Happy Mother's Day, Mom!!

MAY 15: I miss the days when drooling on myself meant I had overserved myself and I had fallen asleep on the couch. As my ALS has progressed, my saliva has increased, which is not as awesome as you might think.

MAY 24: I miss the days when hitting myself in the balls wasn't really a thing I needed to worry about! You see, as my chest muscles die, my shoulders are slowly rotating forward, and as a result, my arms tend to end up in my lap. Considering I now lack the strength to lower my arms gracefully, they tend to just plop down, which can lead to unfortunate consequences!

MAY 26: Of course Chester Copperpot from *The Goonies* had a Lou Gehrig baseball card.

MAY 30: In a scene from the love story *Deadpool* (SPOILER ALERT!) the hero, played brilliantly by Ryan Reynolds, discovers he has cancer. When he decides to leave his true love to shield her from seeing him go through the shit show that cancer can be, he gives the following as his rationale: "The worst part about cancer isn't what it does to you, but what it does to everyone else in your life." And the same applies to ALS. It is simply brutal to see the anguish, sadness, frustration, helplessness, and anger, to name a few emotions, on the faces of my loved ones as I travel on this journey with ALS. I'm so grateful for the tremendous amount of love and support I have from my family and friends, but I'd give anything to be able to shield them from having to see me with this disease. #ALSAwarenessMonth

JUNE 9: Admittedly, I was not familiar with the poem "Invictus" when I received my bracelet inscribed with the title of the poem. I figured it was just a cool bracelet and "Invictus" just meant something badass. Turns out I was right, but that isn't the moral of the story. The moral is that I am the master of my fate, the captain of my soul, and I'm grateful that this bracelet reminds me of that truth.

JUNE 12: I know that people who voted for Donny Little Hands won't read this (because "fake news"), but there is little doubt that all this administration is concerned with is cutting taxes for the wealthiest Americans and is willing to harm our most vulnerable citizens to do so. I didn't ask for ALS. I ate healthily, exercised, and paid my share into Social Security. But now our Least Qualified President in History has determined that the money for SSDI would be better off in the hands of someone else.

JULY 1: Over the past couple of weeks, I have been incredibly fortunate to have been a part of two amazing bike rides. Yet calling them 'rides' isn't exactly giving them their due respect. One is actually a Vision Quest and the other is a Trek through three states. Leisurely bike rides, these are not.

This year was my second Trek. While I'm bummed that I couldn't be at open mic night, it was so inspiring (minus the sunburn) to sit at the end of Tuxis Road and see all the riders come through with their support teams. Sunday was my first time at the top of John Street, which, for those that don't know, has an absolutely brutal hill which some riders attack multiple times. It's also where Emma learned all about Butt Cannons. Even more awesome was knowing that Team Greenwich Police Department were not only riding for Sgt. Roger Petrone, but they were riding for me, too! And the cookout at the finish line is a great chance to be with other PALS, CALS, and the folks at ALS TDI, who are working so tirelessly for a cure.

On the way home, while still on a high from being with so many awesome people, my mind kept drifting back to someone who wasn't even there. Sunday was the anniversary of a horrific accident involving three veterans of the Vision Quest. John Biehn, Tim Ahern, and Graeme Street were all seriously injured that day. A year later, I'm incredibly grateful that Tim and John were able to participate in the third annual Vision Quest.

To be fair, participating undersells John's involvement in the VQ. It's really his brainchild, a ride so gnar and so challenging that you can't help but see a vision or two. He came up with the idea shortly after my diagnosis as a way to raise awareness for ALS and money for me and my family. The third VQ was the best yet, not only in terms of numbers of participants, but also in terms of funds raised! And if I'm being honest, I have no idea how he was able to pull it together when you consider the extensive rehab John had to go through just to walk, let alone ride, AND the fact that John and his equally rad wife, Katie, welcomed Jack, their first son, to their clan in January. John is my brother from another mother, someone who has been there for me, building walls, smoking meat, or helping me understand why you should never miss a Sunday show.

A sincere thank you to this year's Vision Quest, the Tri-State Trek riders, and those that worked behind the scenes to make these events as amazing as they were. You are all amazing. You help give me so much strength. Love you guys!!

SEPTEMBER 17: ALS forced me to make a choice: I could either embrace the beauty and good in my life or wallow in self-pity over what I've lost. I no longer had the time or energy to do both. I'm glad I made the right decision to embrace the good. I am so lucky to have so many great people in my life, and last night was a good reminder of that. Thank you all who made it out last night for a great time. Thank you, Boxty, for the great music. And a huge thank you goes out to everyone who helped make last night possible. From collecting raffle donations to creating tee shirts, it takes a small army to pull off a night like last night. Love you guys, and please remember to embrace the good in your life.

2018

JANUARY 1: Last year was easily the most difficult of my life on a physical, emotional, and spiritual level. I've battled depression and anxiety. I've been lied to, gossiped about, and cast out like an appliance that no longer worked properly.

I'm genuinely grateful for the love and support from family and friends, who have tried their damnedest to keep my head above water, though it feels more like the sunken place if I'm being honest.

That said, I'm going to begin 2018 with a long hiatus from Facebook. My account will remain active, but I won't be on. Best wishes to you and yours for the new year.

JULY 25: Think about all your friends & family who are living with life-threatening diseases or have lost their lives because of those diseases. Now imagine all the good twelve billion dollars could do to aid in that fight.

SEPTEMBER 13: I don't do this nearly as much as I should, but thank you to all the folks who have helped me on this path. ALS can be incredibly isolating and to have so many people in my life who would think to get me Pearl Jam bourbon, Heady Toppers, CBD lotion, or just drop me a text or email helps me remember I'm not alone on this long road. Last week I got to watch my favorite band because of the efforts of some incredible people. Both nights, I got to hang with some of the best people in the world, and that's something I'll never take for granted.

DECEMBER 5: I'm incredibly honored that Jay Picariello would run the Boston Marathon on my behalf to raise money for ALS ONE! I'm fortunate to be able to call Jay a friend for over twenty years, and while I haven't known him to be a distance runner, I know he'll attack his training with the same drive and determination that he's shown since I've known him.

2019

APRIL 16: I was pretty overcome with emotions when Jay approached our spot at the Boston Marathon in Newton. The mixture of emotions and ALS prevented me from telling him how proud I was of him and how grateful I was for his sacrifice and determination in training for, and then running, the Marathon. And while I wasn't able to say how I felt, I think he could tell what I was thinking when he touched my face. I'm so happy this moment was captured. Love you, Jay!

JUNE 11: I wonder if ALS patients are considered the veal of the cannibal community. Routinely I am stretched and massaged and every night have cannabis-infused coconut oil rubbed on my muscles. I bet I'd be delicious.

JULY 15: I love my girls and love my time with them. But I dread the time after I drop them at their mom's place. I dread the feelings of guilt and missing the hell out of them. Sometimes it passes quickly, sometimes it lasts a day or two. But it's always there. Yesterday I wept from the guilt of not being the dad I always thought and hoped I'd be. I hate that ALS has robbed me of the opportunity to be the kind of dad my dad was for me. And there's a lot of guilt that I physically can't make their dinner, can't play cribbage with them, can't shoot hoops with them, can't pick them up when they fall, and can't comfort them when they're sad. I cried because I can't help but feel the loss that they will never know. ❦

ADAPTED FROM THE AUTHOR'S FACEBOOK POSTS

SHELLY HOOVER

Four Pieces

"AN OPEN LETTER TO THE ALS COMMUNITY"

I've lived past my expiration date and I've still got questions.

This month marks five years since my ALS diagnosis with a two-to-five-year prognosis. I've crammed a lifetime of living, loving, learning, and advocating into those few years, and I've still got questions.

I've met hundreds of patients and their families, caregivers, advocates, medical practitioners, researchers, drug developers, regulators, and legislators, and I've still got questions.

Last week, I was reminded at a meeting of people with ALS and FDA regulators that we are all one ALS community. I would agree that we all have a common goal of finding an effective treatment or cure. However, I would argue that we look at the problem though distinct lenses. We champion our own point of view and often dismiss, distrust, or disparage community members who view it through a different lens. We disagree on how to reach the goal at best and cannibalize at worst. I've got some questions about that.

This problem is not new nor unique to the ALS community. But for now, my life and the lives of tens of thousands of other people currently living with ALS depend upon an immediate solution.

The National ALS Association led an effort to create an FDA guidance document to facilitate the clinical trial and drug approval process. It was presented as a collaborative effort, inclusive of all parts of the community. The voice of the conservative neurological science community dominated the conversation and document. Looking through their lens, it was a big win. Looking through my lens, it tragically meant we support the status quo drug approval process which costs $2.5 billion and can stretch out over more than twelve years. That means the research community keeps their version of perfect science while patients like me are guaranteed to die waiting. I understand their position; they are desperately searching for an effective treatment and are unwilling to change because they want that treatment to be scientifically proven. They truly believe that is what's best for patients. Drug developers are looking for an effective treatment as well, and their lens includes dollar signs and a highly regulatory environment. The FDA would be thrilled to approve a treatment that has been proven effective by passing the gold standard of trial design. I want access to potential treatments now. My lens is urgency and access—period.

Can someone please draw a cartoon of this conundrum?

Here's the deal. I, along with many others, have tried to gain traction on pressing for bold changes to this process. Today, I was asked by Sandy, a newly diagnosed woman, "Why isn't something being done? What can I do to create change now?" My heart sank. If I knew what to tell her, I'd be doing it myself. She is one of the lucky ones — participating in a stem cell clinical trial. But, dear God, the study protocols are nothing short of barbaric. Sandy is voluntarily being denied access to currently approved medication for three months to see if she declines rapidly enough to be included in the study. If she progresses enough, she still has a 50% chance of a placebo being surgically injected into her spine. Here's the real kicker: If Sandy gets the stem cells and shows improvement, she will not have access to future treatments for years. Barbaric.

They've got their conservative science that looks promising. Sandy is a desperate, dying woman. She feels it's her responsibility to endure this trial to benefit patients in the future. Can someone please explain to Sandy's family how this is okay? A promising treatment exists but your wife and mother is a lab rat and can't have access to the treatment outside of a barbaric clinical trial.

Nothing is going to change until the patient community demands it. We have to find a solution that creates a win for those of us living with ALS. Let's take an honest look through each other's lenses and find a compelling solution. We need a Manhattan Project funding the brain power and advocacy to make it a reality. Here are my questions:

1) Who has the leadership, resources, and influence to create a win-win for the entire community?

2) What barriers are preventing this from happening now?

I'm sitting in my hospital bed, typing this with my eyes. Yet I believe I can make a difference. What if those with resources and influence acted as though their lives depended upon finding a solution now? The answer is out there. Please help me find it.

"ROLL WITH GRACE"

Death is a constant in the ALS community. Yet this one hit me particularly hard. My dear friend and adopted sister won her battle with ALS on Wednesday, January 18th.

I met Karen and her amazing family in May 2014 at the National ALS Advocacy Days in Washington DC. Instantly, she was my sister from a different mister. She was a few years ahead of me in her ALS progression, yet I knew I wanted to roll with this disease just as she did, with grace and dignity.

Our disease progressions were nearly identical and we would talk and text share the joys of sisterhood and our grief with each new loss. We also shared how thankful we were for our loving husbands who sacrifice so much to take care of us.

I was compelled to emulate her infectious smile and positive attitude. She advocated relentlessly to make life better for people living with ALS.

We looked forward to seeing each other in every year in DC. We even had a surprise meeting at an institute in Florida. Like a true friendship, we would pick up where we left off without missing a beat.

The scientific community is so close to an effective treatment for the SOD1 familial form of ALS that Karen had. I'm angry that she didn't have access to the experimental drug. Yet Karen would tell me to not be angry, it's just the way it is. So, to honor her I won't stay in anger. I'll focus my energy to gratitude for knowing such an amazing woman.

I learned so much from Karen. She set the tone and direction for how I roll in my life with ALS—with grace and dignity.

Here is an excerpt from Karen's final message:

"The day has finally come; I am free from this body that has trapped me. Please don't be sad, celebrate the life that I had before ALS took over. I put up a good fight, and in my mind, I have won my fight against ALS. Yes, this sucks, and I will miss so many great things, but I have had a life filled with love and happiness. ALS could never take away the fact that I have spent many joyous days with the most amazing family and friends. Thank you for making my life such an awesome ride! To my family and friends, thank you for making my life so incredibly awesome. Never forget how fragile life is and that every day matters!"

I'm forgiven and thankful that Karen is Free.

"PREPARING FOR LIFE WITHOUT HANDS"

Legs are relatively easy to replace with equipment and ramps. I use a power chair, shower chair, patient lift, lateral rotation bed, and a van with a ramp and hand controls. Once I'm showered, dressed, and lifted into my power chair—her name is Ruby Tuesday—I have a semblance of independence. I can drive short distances, go to the store, go for a roll, or meet a friend for lunch. This is relatively doable and has been my life for more than three years. Life without working arms and hands is going to be a bit more complicated.

My ALS progression has remained relatively slow. Yet, I've reached a point where I'm losing important function in my arms and hands. Imagine an elastic band wrapped around your chest holding your arms at your sides. Now try to move your elbows away from your body. At the same time, a strong person is pushing down on your shoulders. Now pretend you're eating a bowl of cereal and the same strong person is pushing your hand down while you are trying to reach your mouth. This is what it feels like to move my arms and hands. Simple tasks like putting a jacket on and off or brushing my hair are difficult, if not impossible, and physically exhausting. I've limited my driving to only a few miles during the day. I haven't had any close calls while driving but I'm being proactive and not taking a chance of having an accident caused by fatigue.

I watch my two-year-old grandson gradually master the use of his hands. As an infant, he would try to grasp a toy or reflexively grab my finger. Then he could pick up a Cheerio and find his mouth. Now he can manipulate puzzle pieces and draw circles with a crayon. As my hands atrophy and lose function, we are traveling the same path in opposite directions. We will meet soon on the continuum.

Tasks requiring fine motor skills are eluding me. I can't open a shampoo bottle or squeeze a tube of toothpaste. Eating in public is quite embarrassing as I eat like a toddler hoping the finger food makes it into my mouth on the first attempt. Last night I tried to put a handful of vitamins and meds into my mouth, like I do every night, and completely missed. Not one pill made it to my mouth. So, I tried again successfully with a two-handed approach.

Like the equipment that replaces my legs, I have some new technology that will replace my hands…

Meet Tobii. Tobii is a speech-generating device that can be controlled with my eyes. The bar below the screen has a camera that follows the reflection of light from my retinas. My eyes move the cursor like a mouse. I can navigate in the apps provided, make a phone call, use any Microsoft program, or access the world wide web. Pretty amazing! Tobii joined the family a few weeks ago. There's quite a learning curve to achieve proficiency and I want to make that happen before I'm completely dependent upon it. For now, I can still type with my shaking fingers, but my days of typing over 100 wpm are long gone. So, I practice typing with my eyes in the evening when my hands need to rest.

Meet Obi. I met Obi the robotic feeding arm last week. We practiced by eating Cheerios and it was love at first bite. My occupational therapist is helping me make Obi a permanent part of the family. She is also working on a voice-activated control for my bed so I can operate the 13 functions without using the remote. I'm forever grateful to the VA healthcare system that generously provides all my technology and equipment. Thanks to the VA, I am able to live the healthiest, safest, most engaged, and independent life possible. Many people with ALS rely on Medicare and do not have access to this life-giving technology.

The past few months have been emotionally difficult as I process the grief of my diminishing independence. Spontaneous tears. Racing thoughts bounce in my head:

I don't want to live anymore.

I can do this with the support of my husband, family, and friends.

I want to quit everything and hide.

I can stay engaged in teaching and writing.

I'm a burden to my husband and children.

How will I cope with total paralysis?

Then I noticed that my thoughts are all about me and this self-focus is not emotionally healthy. It's time to return to gratitude, be present, and engage at whatever level I can at the moment.

I'm forgiven and free and grateful for my family and technology.

"UNMET EXPECTATIONS"

Much of my emotional suffering is a result of unmet expectations.

The visible suffering of ALS is obvious in loss of ability to control my body. Sure, it's frustrating for me and everyone who loves me. So, we slow down, add equipment, change routines, adapt, and adjust.

We all have expectations, beliefs, that something is likely to happen.

Get out of bed. Walk to the kitchen. Pour a cup of coffee.

Most able-bodied people wake every morning knowing these things will happen. It's expected. Even though I can visualize myself doing these simple tasks, I have no expectation that they are going to happen without assistance. Acceptance lessens suffering.

Having unreasonable expectations is a great source of suffering.

The key to limiting suffering? Reframe expectations of myself and others. Let me explain. I suffered a great deal the past six months because of what was happening politically in the U.S. I was physically and emotionally sick. I quit writing, I changed political parties, I quit my Bible study, I unfollowed friends on Facebook and was unfollowed and unfriended by a great deal more. I spiraled. I was horrified at the thought of a greedy, narcissistic, degrading, mocking, lying bully being elected President and didn't want to be around anyone or any organization who did. I expected others to view the election as I did, to see what I saw, and to value what I valued. Didn't happen. My expectations, what I believed was likely to happen, didn't happen. I suffered for it. Tremendously.

I was wrong for placing my expectations on others.

I've thought through the angst I caused myself and have reframed my expectations. Am I happy and accepting of the election results? Unequivocally no. But I have removed the unreasonable expectation that others view the world as I do. I'm channeling my energy to promote issues of social justice and compassion. A much better choice than suffering.

Here's another example: I expect my family and friends to read my mind, to know what I'm thinking, and to know what I need from them. Nonsensical. When I find myself suffering because of what someone else is doing or not doing, I have to stop and ask: Do I have a reasonable expectation? Have I communicated my need? If the answer is no, I am causing my own suffering.

Does this practice eliminate all of my emotional pain? No. The feelings are real and I have to find a way to process them. However, I do have a sense of controlling how long and to what depth I experience the pain. I'm able to roll away from it when I'm done.

What can we reasonably expect from others?

I'm not suggesting we all walk away from relationships and disengage from society. But I am suggesting that we carefully examine the judgment and expectations we place on others. What can I reasonably expect? I expect to be treated with care and respect and will reciprocate in kind. However, I have no expectation that you will be able to read my mind or think or act the way I expect you to. If someone doesn't treat me with care and respect, I can choose to not be in a relationship with him or her. If that's not an option, I can emotionally disengage.

Are you the cause of your own suffering?

What are you expecting from people or society that is causing you to suffer? We have no right to expect justice or deference. Really, we don't. So, take a step towards eliminating your own suffering and finding freedom by reframing your expectations.

I'm forgiven and free and reframing my expectations. 🐾

DAVID O'NAN

Are We Just Shade?

a fever of the mind to inspire artwork

There is a factory
machines, other deities, control—
moulding bones from lost souls.
We are possibly cut from the same skin fabric
wrapped around our skeletons straight from this factory
And distributed around the world as humans.
Possible?
As we learn what we are
the muscles develop like magic—
the heart, the brain, the lungs
are injected into us as a seed of ink, or blood
to sprout amongst us as our energy, form us
into breath, into pain, into love,
into sanity or insanity, into beauty,
into dreamers, into light, into shade. ❧

COREY POLEN

A Hoosier ALS Journey

JANUARY 17

I know it has been awhile since I have posted an update. So here it goes.

I am astonished by the continuous support. From family members to neighbors to colleague friends to grade-school friends to college friends to Brownsburg friends to families of sport teams to friends of friends to people I don't even know: thank you from the bottom of my heart. Every donation has helped and we are extremely gracious of your kindness.

I officially started the clinical trial on December 14th. I won't get into the details of what it is, but I receive a daily injection for thirty-six weeks. It's a phase III trial, which means it's testing for effectiveness. It is also a double-blinded, placebo-controlled trial. Which means, there is a fake treatment and neither the researchers nor the participants know until the study is over. To be honest, I've been on the medication for 1 month and I've had no side-effects. Based on the medication, I would expect some specific side effects. Even if I'm on the placebo, that is part of the process in moving things forward. Unfortunately, this will likely be my last clinical trial. There is typically a set of onset criteria for ALS clinical trials. I barely made the current trial I'm on. I will have "aged-out" of most new trials, since I've had symptoms for longer than two years.

I've also recently finished my driver's training. I gained the skills required quickly. I guess all those years of video games finally paid off. My reward is that now I can't drive until I have a modified vehicle. I'm in the process of trying to accomplish that. Additionally, I expect to have my first wheelchair soon. I had hoped to have it by now, but I won't get into too many details. In short, the FDA had created some barriers for manufacturers for certain specialized parts I required.

I also participated in a press conference for a proposed bill in the Indiana House, HB 1157. It received a lot of media attention. I have heard from many people who pour their hearts out to me in support. I have done all I can do. It is up to each citizen to contact their legislator, Brian Bosma, and Governor Holcomb to have your voice heard.

All in all, I'm doing fine. Things are moving forward. I'm moving forward and excited for spring to arrive.

MAY 10

Hey everyone. I know it has been a while since my last update. You can all rest easy, though. I've been really happy just living life. Spring is a very busy time for the Polen household. I am extremely happy for this warmer weather.

First off, I cannot say it enough: thank you for each and every donation. The additional expenses due to this disease are immense. Every donation helps out.

The home remodel is complete. However, we are still in the process of modifying the garage entry so that I can enter the house. I will require a lift for my wheelchair. Unfortunately, this takes time to achieve. I had a couple bad falls about a month ago. Luckily, after an MRI, I did not break or tear anything in my knee. Extremely painful though, but that should subside in a few more weeks. The lift will be very helpful. Currently, my amazing wife helps me into the house. It's not a pretty process. However, I fear that I will accidentally hurt her one day, so the ramp can't come soon enough. Nowadays, I use a wheelchair when I'm not in the house. It took some getting used to. I'm very relieved though, knowing that I won't fall from walking and need the help of strangers to get back on my feet.

Our van has now been converted into a wheelchair accessible vehicle. This means I can officially drive again. I was beginning to like being chauffeured around. Having the independence again is nice, though. I'm getting used to everything taking me longer to do. I think God is telling me I need to work on my patience. I'm still on my clinical trial. No real developments there. I'm on week twenty-two. I still think I'm on the placebo and still hate the injections.

All in all, I'm doing better than I should be this far into the disease. I'm very grateful for my health even though I'm definitely weaker than last time I posted. Our oldest son will be graduating high school soon and heading to college. When I was first diagnosed, I didn't think I'd make it to see this. Now, I am hoping to be able to see the same for our second child in a couple years.

Thank you for the continued love, prayers, and support. Oh, and thanks for making it to the new site. Feel free to share it.

AUGUST 27

Hello avid followers, friends, colleagues, and family. I don't want to inundate you with numerous updates. So, I'm trying to keep a happy medium.

I'm still working on acquiring a lift. I've also started the process of trying to get a powered wheelchair. My legs are extremely weak and entrance into and out of our home is very risky to me and my family. I've fallen several times recently but my family is always there to help lift me up, physically and emotionally. Knowing what I once was capable of is really hard. I miss being able to "do" and "accomplish" things for my family. I've always been hands on, and now all I find myself focusing on are things I cannot do but used to be able to. This disease impacts the whole family. I have to be the luckiest guy for how my family has persevered through the never-ending challenges. I love them all so much.

I'm officially off my 36-week double-blinded trial. Now, I am on "open-label" for forty-eight weeks. The medication is no cure for ALS. However, it's an option to "stay stronger longer." Not a lot of optimism, but it is all science will allow me to have. There are many setbacks with this disease, but one I did not fathom was the cruel timeline for clinical trials. Getting diagnosed for ALS takes typically twelve to eighteen months from initial onset. Once that occurs, you are eligible for the ALS clinics, which also means you can start entering clinical trials. Well, enrollment in a trial itself takes months if you meet all the criteria. Most of the "good trials" require onset of fewer than twenty-four months as to not taint the results with your 'lucky health'. So, most patients will get access to maybe one trial. If you're geographically lucky, you might have access to one "good trial" like NurOwn. I've now aged out of the system with my 'great health'. Additionally, clinical trial sponsors complain they don't have enough patients for their trials. I'm astonished at how really smart people cannot connect these two dots.

The Right to Try law: People close to me always knew I was not in favor of this law. Patients already have "access" to medications under EAP, the Enhanced Access Plan. However, the road block was not the government. It was Pharma. They stated too much risk, so RTT was created to remove those barriers. However, RTT does not require Pharma to give patients access to medication. Both have the same roadblock that no one was willing to breach. It's *cost*. Pharma must supply the medication at the cost to manufacture it (no profit). While you might think this is great, Pharma is *for profit.* Releasing a cost structure would jeopardize their future profits. I understand both sides. The thing that should trouble people is how this was "sold" to the American public. President Trump, Vice President Pence, Senator Joe Donnelly (Indiana), and even Chaim Lebovits (CEO and President of BrainStorm) all rode the publicity train at the expense of terminally ill patients, providing no true solution to access. To throw salt on a wound, BrainStorm dragged ALS patients through conference calls raising hope of the RTT path. During this free publicity tour, investors were very present, offering more questions than patients. In the end, BrainStorm secured $12 million before resolutely shutting down a path for RTT patients.

In the seventy-nine years since Lou Gehrig stamped his name on this disease only two medications have come to market. There is hope on the horizon with NurOwn, ALS TDI, and CRISPR, but there is no sense of urgency when it comes to this disease. Being around it for a couple years makes you see how many companies run this as a business rather than truly finding a solution. Sadly, one of those companies is the ALS Association. While they do some great things, they are also sitting on a huge investment account due to the Ice Bucket Challenge from a few years ago. And now they are trying to ramp it back up, just to build the investment account higher. The ALS National Registry is another money pit. Their sole goal was to measure prevalence, yet more than $80 million later they still struggle to achieve that goal. To be honest, I think the lack of urgency is due to the short life span of this disease. Those that can fight only have so much time to fight the system. Then there is a new set of patients that must learn what's happening. It's an evil cycle that is just waiting for someone to buck the trend. Waiting for a scientist to take the risk. ALS patients are guaranteed failure if we won't take the risk.

OCTOBER 12

Current Status: First things first, I'm doing okay. The Polens made it through summer and the kids are back to school. We even successfully got one of them off to college. I'm so proud of each of them, as well as my beautiful wife. They each amaze me every day. They constantly take on a bigger role every day than the day before. This terrible disease takes a lot from us. However, I've also seen that it provides many learning opportunities for our family. For that, I am grateful. Being able to see them tackle new challenging tasks brings me great comfort.

Happenings: I have made the choice to go off the open-label trial I was on. The side effects were just too great and it was providing me zero benefits. I hope it works for other ALS patients, but for me it does not. Next week my power wheelchair arrives.

Luck: If I didn't have bad luck I wouldn't have any luck. The lift for me in my garage is *finally* complete. I was told it would take three days. It took over six weeks from beginning to end. Anything that could go wrong, did. From load-bearing studs to a missing part taking two weeks to arrive, many things wreaked havoc. At times I couldn't leave the house and was unable to go into work. I'm glad it's over with though. It's one less thing that provides the opportunity for me to hurt myself, or worse yet, someone I love.

Thoughts: My recent trial is a great example of what's wrong with ALS trials and the FDA. I was on the placebo for thirty-six weeks. I then received open-label access to the medication. It took me about six weeks—four on, two dosing down—to realize the side effects were too much and it wasn't helping me. That means during the prime of my ability to do a clinical trial, it stole forty-two weeks from me. Forty-two weeks of an illness that typically doesn't last longer than three years. That time does not include selecting a trial as well as the time to start the trial. I was able to have open-label access but many trials don't even provide that. Additionally, now I won't qualify for most other trials due to "aging out." This got me thinking about how the FDA was a roadblock for AIDS back in the 1980s, and how one patient, Ron Woodroof, changed that landscape by not accepting the "standard of care" protocol. ALS is in this boat and has been for at least eighty years. I can't accept this terrible standard of care.

Coincidentally, it was recently the thirtieth anniversary of ACT UP's "Seize Control of the FDA" event. AIDS patients/protesters staged a "die-in" featuring tombstone placards critical of the FDA. Bringing the AIDS vs. FDA fight to the forefront of discussions brought real change to the FDA process of terminally ill AIDS patients. ALS needs our own Ron Woodroof. Is that me? I don't know. That is what has been consuming my thoughts of late.

I do know this: if I'm going to die from this dreaded disease then I want to die *trying*. I don't want to die from a placebo, or being protected to death. ALS patients are guaranteed failure if we won't take the risk. Every time I've tried to gain access under the Right to Try law, I've been denied. I actually can't find any ALS patient that had success in the five months and more of its status as a law. This leads me to believe that Right to Try should be relabeled as Right to Die, though Death with Dignity Laws are much more compassionate than RTT.

Thank you for the continued love, prayers, and support. Thanks for reading and please feel free to share. ❧

ADAPTED FROM THE AUTHOR'S 2018 WEBSITE POSTS

CATHERINE SCOTT

In My Dreams

In my dreams
I walk along unassisted,
breathing air deep into my lungs
without having to be connected to a ventilator.

In my dreams
I smell the saltiness of the ocean
and the fragrance of flowers in full bloom.

In my dreams
I devour my favorite foods by actually eating them,
enjoying exquisite explosions of flavor in my mouth.

In my dreams
I am not disabled.
In my dreams
I do not have ALS.

My dreams are a bittersweet reminder of what it was like
before that fateful spring day all those years ago
when I received the diagnosis that changed my life.

Is it kindness or cruelty that my physical wholeness
is reflected only when I sleep?
I don't know.

I do know that the decision of how I perceive
these dream moments is entirely up to me.
I choose to see them for what they are…
as *dreams*, and not nightmares.
As precious reminders of what my life was once like,
and reminders of the possibilities
a cure could bring in the future.

I Am Enough

I am nearly paralyzed with little movement
ascribed to my own efforts, and yet
I am enough.

I rely on man-made medical equipment to eat
and to breathe, and yet
I am enough.

Even on days when I feel unwell or emotionally down,
I am enough.

Our worth is not the manifestation of what we are able to physically
accomplish. It is, rather, the simple act of being—the determination
to do all that we possibly can with what we have to work with;
to be of service to the world and all of God's creations
who occupy it; to love and be kind.

I am enough. &.

JAY SMITH

Divorce or Death?
A Real Life Decision

WHEN I WAS DIAGNOSED, I WAS GIVEN TWO YEARS TO LIVE. Two-and-a-half years later here I am typing this article using my eyes, while being fed through a tube in my stomach and wearing a breathing mask to give my diaphragm a break. I am one of the lucky ones, and I'm thankful for that.

I still think about how awesome it would be to be sitting at bar in a divey Mexican restaurant with my wife, shoveling way too many salty chips and chasing them down with cheap margaritas. I'd be happier than a truck driver after an eight-hour stretch to be able to scratch my balls again, but I digress. You might be surprised that the hardest thing about ALS isn't trying to vigorously type in a witty, timely jab with eyes when your buddy does something stupid. It is the cost to stay alive.

When I was diagnosed I came across other patients, like Eric Valor, who through mechanical ventilation has been able to stay alive for over ten years. Then there's Augie Nieto who has been very actively fighting this beast for twelve years and is the current Chairman of the board at ALS.net. And of course, we all know Stephen Hawking, who I like to tell people I have the same disease as to make me seem smarter. I mean, I bet we both share the burning desire to scratch our balls, so there's that.

It's estimated that the care for an ALS patient is over $200,000 a year. I ran my own company for ten years and while I always chose a new hire over a pay raise, I was able to bring in enough to convince my wife to "give it another year." I put away a few thousand dollars each year into my retirement and paid my fair share into Social Security, both as an employee and employer. So, when I could no longer work because of ALS, I applied for Social Security Disability and Medicare. When I found out that I would only collect around $20,000 a year, we thought, okay, my wife will go back to work and Medicare will cover the medical expenses. I was wrong, almost dead wrong.

I now require a full-time caretaker while my wife is at work, which is not covered by insurance. As my breathing continues to decline, I can extend my life for a very long time with a tracheotomy and ventilator, but at what cost? I will require round-the-clock care, more sophisticated technology, not to mention a $30,000 used wheelchair-accessible minivan, none of which are covered by Medicare. There are government programs to help cover these costs, but not for middle class families. So, my choices are to give up everything and declare bankruptcy, divorce my wife, or just accept death.

Fellow ALS patient Eric Valor describes the cost of staying alive: "First and foremost, it cost me my marriage. I lost my house and all my savings. I am now destitute, living solely on Social Security, most of which goes to partially pay for my 24/7 care team. The majority of that bill is picked up by Medicaid (not Medicare), for which I must have no assets in order to qualify. ALS took me from a top 10% wage earner to below poverty level."

Catherine Scott, the mother of Anthony Carbajal whose 2014 Ice Bucket Challenge video helped it become a viral sensation, and who also shares the same disease as her son, explains the financial deviation. "It takes everything. After paying all of our monthly obligations it takes every single discretionary dollar we have left to keep me at home by paying for a caretaker out of our own pockets… and even then, we fall short about $1,200 per month." Catherine, whose ability to breathe on her own is coming to an end, will also be faced with my decision.

In Japan, the life expectancy for someone with ALS is much longer than in the United States. Not because of their fish-centered diets or their awesome martial arts movies, but because over ninety percent opt for a tracheotomy to dramatically extend their lives compared to the only five percent here in the US. It simply comes down to costs. The Japanese government provides support for its citizens with this devastating disease and ours doesn't. As the most advanced country in the world, we have to do better. A thirty-eight-year-old father of two who ran his own business, I should not be penalized by being middle class, but I am. I shouldn't have to decide between divorce and death, but I have to. ❧

FOUR SEASONS

AN ART PORTFOLIO
BY SEEROON YERETZIAN

BORN IN 1951 AT THE TIRO REFUGEE CAMP IN LEBANON, Seeroon Yeretzian received her BA in Fine Arts in 1985 from the Otis-Parsons Art Institute and School of Design. She has authored four books—her self-titled art album, *Seeroon Yeretzian*; a book of poetry, *Word Weaving & Black Seat Confessions*; the best-selling *Seeroon Darer: Armenian Ornate Initials*, which served as artistic inspiration for an award-winning float design for the 126th Annual Rose Parade; and her latest, *Evolution is My Revolution: Woven Words and Vivid Dreams*, which she wrote after her ALS diagnosis using the DynaVox eye-tracking device. Throughout her life, Seeroon has encountered both beauty and suffering in the world. This dichotomy manifests artistically in what she calls her "Sunshine" and "Moonshine" series. The "Sunshine" pieces are rich in color, showcasing life-giving earthly elements. By contrast the "Moonshine" works reflect themes based on personal experiences ranging from the Armenian Genocide to homelessness and self-identity. Recognized for reviving the art of ancient Armenian petroglyphs and medieval Armenian ornamental art, her masterpieces include the alphabets of seventeen different languages executed in the tradition and style of traditional Armenian ornate initials.

Seeroon has exhibited in numerous solo and group shows and her art is found in private collections and major institutions. In 2014, the City of Glendale, California bestowed upon her its "Lifetime Achievement Award" for the arts. Find more of her work at www.seeroonart.com. 🦋

Above: "Spring" - Below: "Summer"

Above: "Autumn" - Below: "Winter"

KIERAN WHITE

Life Isn't Fair

My Journey as a Young Caregiver

THE MEMORY BLURS AS TIME PASSES BY, BUT NEVER REALLY goes away. I remember sitting at my little desk watching videos on the computer, completely engrossed in them. I was nine years old. It was the summer of 2012 in Nicoya, Costa Rica.

My mom and I were on a vacation in her home country. Everything seemed so simple and routine. Life is always an easy routine, until it's not. The most pressing issue on my mind was which video game I was going to ask my parents for when I got home.

I was startled by the noise of people sobbing outside the room. I made my way to the living room, hesitant but curious. My mom and three of her sisters were there. A bunch of other cousins and friends were scattered around the house. Over all of the noise, I could still hear the crying. I saw my mom and aunts sobbing, holding each other. I was immediately confused. What was going on? And I was distracted by the smell of the food being prepared in the kitchen.

I hobbled over to my mom, grabbed her shoulder, and asked her what was going on. Her response was the classic parental comeback when something is definitely wrong: "Nothing honey, everything is fine." That would have been pretty easy to believe, if it wasn't for all the crying. I said okay and went back to my videos. How out of the ordinary it was to see my family crying. But I wanted to use the computer some more.

That incident was mostly ignored for a couple of months after we returned home. I can't believe I spent all that time completely oblivious to how my life had been changed forever.

Life went on, and everything seemed fine. I remember sitting on our back porch one day, talking to my dad about something. He said it wasn't fair to keep me in the dark, and asked my mom to sit outside with us. I had no idea what was going on, having almost completely forgotten the Costa Rica episode a few months earlier. Being told that you've been kept in the dark is like being told that you are too naive to realize what is happening behind the scenes of your own life. I felt the warm summer air on my skin, but that wasn't what made me sweat. I was going to be told something that would change my life, my perception of the world, and the very person I had grown to be up until then.

Calmly and gently, my dad told me that he had been diagnosed with a serious and eventually fatal disease called amyotrophic lateral sclerosis, or ALS. He explained that over the next few years, he would lose his ability to move his arms and legs, then lose basically all of his muscle mass, and eventually be unable to talk or breathe. I felt as though I was in some sort of science-fiction movie. How could you go from a perfectly healthy adult to an immobile shell of your former self in just a few years? I didn't understand exactly what that would look like until I was shown a picture of Stephen Hawking, the British physicist who was diagnosed with ALS at the age of twenty-one. My parents tried to comfort me by explaining that he had had ALS for more than fifty years, and that cases vary from person to person. They explained that dad could live for more than the two-to-five-year life expectancy. Or less.

I remember feeling so overwhelmed I couldn't comprehend anything being said to me. I felt tears moisten my eyes. I was speechless. I spent the rest of that week dealing with what had just trampled my life as I knew it. My dad was my best friend, my greatest role model, my favorite person to be around. How could I watch him shrivel into a smaller shell of his former self? He was always larger than life and invincible in my eyes. I didn't know. Maybe I still don't.

After the revelation, I fell into a depression. I couldn't think about anything else. I began to wonder about the afterlife, about existence itself, about how a cure could be found during his lifetime. I remember we went to Disney World, "the happiest place on earth," and feeling like nothing else mattered anymore. If my greatest hero, my dad, was taken away from me, what would I be reduced to? The answers I sought were scattered around the chapters of my life. I have found some answers but there are others I may never stop seeking. This portion of my life really hurt. There's no other word for it. Part of me felt damaged during that time. But like my dad always says, "Life isn't fair." Why should I have expected it to be?

In these seven years, some aspects of my life got easier, others not so much. Through the grace of God, my dad is still with us today, "alive and kicking," as he likes to say. I am now one of his primary caregivers, along with my mom, who pretty much runs the whole show. Dad has lost all of his strength in both arms, and can only walk with assistance. He is now totally dependent on me and my mom. A whole world of responsibility fell on me.

There have been ups and downs along the way. But I'd be lying if I said nothing good has come out of it. I truly feel that because of my dad's diagnosis, I have become a better person. I have grown in empathy and compassion towards others, and I can put myself into other people's shoes better than if I had lived a more happy-go-lucky lifestyle.

I was forced to grow up fast, and because of that, I have become more mature. I believe that from suffering comes wisdom. I'm not claiming to be Yoda. I've developed as a human being *because* of what I've gone through.

From this new sense of maturity and compassion, I have also found ways to serve a purpose greater than myself. During the past seven years, my family and I have participated in many fundraising opportunities to support efforts to cure ALS. We've become advocates. We joined the annual Walk to Defeat ALS. We attended the ALS Advocacy Conference in Washington. We have shared our story in videos and newspaper articles. No matter how small a role we play to help eradicate the disease, it feels good to do our part for a cause near and dear to our hearts.

As far as caregiving goes, I spend a lot of my time during the day assisting my dad with his daily needs. I have been taught how to help him maintain as good a quality of life as possible. I've learned how to do a daily range of motion exercises, how to use a variety of equipment such as braces and breathing machines, and how to assist him in getting into his wheelchair, his bed, and the car. Despite needing help with pretty much everything he does, my dad has shown an incredible amount of resilience in maintaining a positive attitude and sense of humor. His situation undoubtedly takes a toll on his mental state, but he never fails to be the goofball in the room who puts a smile on everyone's face. His positivity is contagious. I am lifted up when I see him appreciate life so much, even under these circumstances. His favorite line to say is, "I have Lou Gehrig's disease, and I wish I could give it back to him."

Despite everything, the least I can say is that I'm happy. Sometimes, it makes me sad when I think my dad may not be here for the special moments of my life—my college graduation, my wedding, and my firstborn. But then I find comfort knowing that my dad lives inside of me, I am an extension of him, and he will forever be in my heart.

To other young caregivers who stumble upon my story, I want you to know that it gets better. Any sadness you feel will subside. Your uncertainty will teach you important lessons, and your courage in the darkest of times is what will keep you going till the end. Make of that what you will, and good luck as you navigate your own journey. ❧

About Our Contributors

Ady **BARKAN** is the founding director of two major projects—Local Progress and the Fed Up campaign—at the Center for Popular Democracy. His current work is focused on strengthening America's health care system, and in organizing and motivating Americans to protect democracy from racism and kleptocracy. Before joining CPD, Ady was a law clerk in the Southern District of New York and a team member at Make the Road New York, representing workers in the recovery of unpaid wages, collective action, and advocacy for safe and dignified working conditions. He helped design and draft policy proposals to enhance the quality of low-wage jobs in New York City including the right to paid sick days, regulation of major retailers, and unionization of the car wash industry. He is a graduate of Yale Law School and Columbia College. Find him online at www.adybarkan.com and on Twitter @adybarkan.

Richard **BEDLACK** went to college at William and Mary in Virginia for his undergraduate education and earned his MD and PhD at the Univer-

sity of Connecticut before relocating to Duke
University for his internship, residency and fel-
lowship years. He is currently a professor of neurology and director of the Duke ALS Clinic. He
has won awards for teaching, patient care, and
activism, including the American Academy of
Neurology Patient Advocate of the Year and the
Rasmussen ALS Patient Advocate of the Year. He

has published more than a hundred articles concerning ALS. He is a leader
of ALSUntangled, a program which utilizes social networking to investigate
alternative and off-label treatment options, as well as of ALS Reversals, a
project attempting to understand why some people with ALS recover from
it and how to make this happen more often. He lives in Durham, North Car-
olina with his wife Shelly and their two mischievous cats.

Joseph E. **BOLTON** and his brother Davy grew
up in North Attleboro, Massachusetts along with
siblings Peter, Charlene, Patrick and loving parents Carol and Joseph. Retiring after twenty-five
years in the Army (including one combat tour
in Afghanistan) Joseph now lives in Leominster,
Massachusetts. An avid skier, hiker and swim-
mer, Joseph loves exploring the New England

wilderness with his wife Mary and his daughters Rachel and Lydia. His latest book, *La Troupe de Sabots: A French-Canadian Folktale*, is available on

Amazon. Inspired by his brother's heroic struggle with ALS, Joseph created the blog www.au-
gustinesalley.wordpress.com as a way to share his
brother's story.

Daniel **CAMPBELL** is thirteen years old and
lives in California with his mom and two older
brothers. His father passed away from ALS in

April of 2018. His spoken word poem in this anthology is the production of collaboration with
poet and writer Wendy Angulo.

Kyle **CONNORS** was diagnosed with ALS in
the autumn of 2014. A proud father of two won-
derful daughters, he was fortunate to be cared for
by his incredible parents until his passing.

Holly **COOPER** lives in Oakland, California,
and works as an editor and digital content writer.
She was the primary caregiver for Michael Thomson—the love of her life—for most of his battle
with ALS. Holly and Mike met in 2008 and were
together for three years. They never stopped loving each other and remained friends until Mike's
diagnosis in 2018, when they reunited. Connect
with her on Twitter @hollycooper333.

Sarah **EZEKIEL** was diagnosed with motor
neuron disease at the age of thirty-four. She has
served as Secretary of the NW London Branch
of the MND Association since 2012 and is now
co-chair. Sarah is also a patron of the charity Life-
lites, which provides life-enhancing technology
to children's hospices. Sarah was honored as the

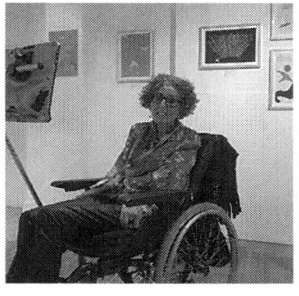

Third Sector Volunteer of the Year in 2016. Using DynaVox eyegaze technology, art software and a Tobii PCEye, Sarah creates paintings which have
been exhibited all over the UK and in Qatar. She has featured in national
news publications and on BBC Radio, *London Tonight*, and *Inside Out*. Connect with her online at www.sarahezekiel.com or via Etsy @EzekielArtShop.

Angelina **FANOUS** was born in Giza, Egypt, and moved to the USA with
her family when she was ten years old. After earning her BA in magazine
journalism at Syracuse University, she was working as a writer and report-

er when she was diagnosed with ALS in 2014. She spent the following year producing a documentary for *VICE* on HBO about ALS and the shortcomings of the federal approval process for treatments for neurodegenerative diseases. Her work has appeared in *The New York Times*, *New York* magazine's *The Cut*, *Vulture*, and *GrubStreet*. She lives in Ohio with her parents and spends her

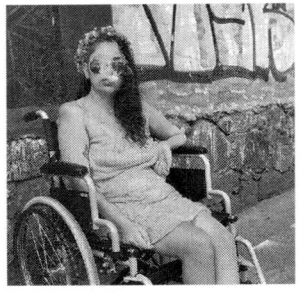

days planning off-roading adventures in her wheelchair. She's traveled to Iceland, the Sierra Norte mountains in Oaxaca, Mexico, and Chilean Patagonia. Find her on Twitter @notsovanilla. (Photo by Danielle Silverman.)

Shelly **HOOVER** earned her EdD at Sacramento State University. She retired from school administration in 2013 when diagnosed with ALS at age forty-seven. She lives in Northern California with her husband Steve; their two grown children and four grandchildren live nearby. Shelly is a Navy veteran, an author, a research ambassador, and an advocate. Writing her blog serves as a tool

to process the losses ALS brings and as a vehicle to steer herself and others toward gratitude. Connect with her online at www.shellyhoover.com or on Twitter @shellyhoover. Her debut novel *Timeless Sisters: Peace at the River* is available on Amazon.

Norman **MACISAAC** used to travel the world supporting local efforts to fight poverty and injustice, before ALS turned his world upside down. He has lived and worked in Africa, Latin America, and Asia. He has been a leader in the field of international development and a critical voice arguing against top-down development. His 2019

TED Talk explored parallels between ALS and international development, highlighting the potential of local initiatives and authentic grassroots voices in the struggle for a more just world. His 2019 book, *The Best of the Worst News: Tales of Inspiration from Around the World and My Life with ALS*, intertwines autobiographical tales spanning five continents.

Osiel **MENDOZA** was born and raised in Martinez, California and is the youngest of three siblings. Pursuing his passion for sports, he ventured to the University of Oregon after high school to earn a degree in Sports Business and Nonprofit Management. He was diagnosed with ALS during his senior year at Oregon, at the age of twenty-one. Thereafter he became an avid ALS advocate. Osiel currently lives in Sonoma County, California with his wife Bella and their golden retriever Hendrix. His speech in this anthology was originally delivered at the ALS TDI White Coat Affair in 2017; the photo here shows him at that event.

David **O'NAN** grew up in Western Kentucky, New Orleans, and Los Angeles, and currently resides in Evansville, Indiana. A creative writer and winner of several spoken word contests, he has read in venues throughout Southern Indiana & Western Kentucky including featured reader spots for poetry honoring John Lennon and Jeff Buckley, and the works of Bukowski, Plath, Sexton, Kerouac, Frost, and Eliot. His books including *The Famous Poetry Outlaws Are Painting Walls and Whispers* (2021) and *The Cartoon Diaries* (2019) are available on Amazon. He is Editor-in-Chief of *Fevers of the Mind Poetry Digest* and a contributor to *Avalanches in Poetry: Writings and Art Inspired by Leonard Cohen*. He has been fundraising for ALS since his father was diagnosed with the ailment in 2016, working with the ALS Association and the ALS Therapy Development Institute. Find him on Twitter @davidlonan1.

Corey **POLEN** is from Brownsburg, Indiana. He and his wife have been married for more than twenty years and have three children together. He works as an information management consultant for a leading actuarial consulting firm. He advocates for ALS on many fronts so that the next generation of patients has fewer obstacles to face and can look ahead to a better outcome than those fighting today. Connect with him on Twitter @CoreyPolen.

Ron **SCHAFFER** was born in Missouri and raised in Rockford, Illinois. As a former engineer for Georgia-Pacific, Ron oversaw capital projects and was responsible for turning failing plants into profit centers. He contracted ALS at the age of fifty-seven, and has lived with the disease for nearly two decades. For those recently diagnosed, Ron would say: "Don't listen to the one-to-three-year rhetoric. Live each day as it comes. Stay busy and do not give in."

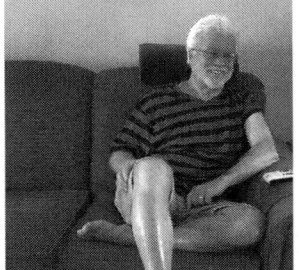

Catherine **SCOTT** had a successful career in project management for the emergency services industry before retiring after receiving an ALS diagnosis in 2002. She currently serves as a member of the Board of Directors for Team Gleason and is a passionate advocate for the ALS community.

Jay **SMITH** is a father, husband, and son living with ALS. Prior to his diagnosis he was the founder and principal of the Austin-based music tech company Livid Instruments. Jay currently runs his foundation Every90Minutes, raising awareness and funds for ALS research. He writes

for *Huffington Post* and on his own popular Facebook blog. Jay enjoys developing new technology to enable people with disabilities to lead more productive and independent lives. Connect with him online at www.facebook.com/Every90Minutes, on Twitter @every90mins and Instagram @every-90minutes.

Michael **THOMSON** was diagnosed with ALS in 2018. Born in Vietnam, he grew up in Houston and Southern California, then trained in the Navy as a combat medic and surgical technician. Mike was honorably discharged after receiving injuries in an explosion during a training exercise. He went on to attend the University of California, Berkeley, graduating with a degree in integrative biology, then lived in Hawaii and New York City before returning to the San Francisco area. He volunteered extensively and enjoyed writing, surfing, playing guitar, and reading organic chemistry textbooks for fun. Mike passed away in 2019 at the age of forty-eight. Learn more about his life and find more of his writing at www.phoenixmichael.com.

Francis **TSAI** was a prominent American comic book artist, illustrator, author, and conceptual artist. He was of Taiwanese and Japanese ancestry. Learn more about his artwork at www.teamgt.com.

Brian **WALLACH** is an attorney and ALS patient. In the aftermath of his diagnosis in 2017, he and his wife founded I AM ALS, a patient-led, patient-centric movement to lead the fight for a cure to the disease. Wallach is an associate at the law firm Skadden, Arps, Slate, Meagher & Flom LLP. From 2014 to 2018, he served as an assistant

United States attorney in the Northern District of Illinois. From 2011 to 2013, he was senior vetting counsel in the Obama White House, overseeing the vetting process for nearly all Senate-confirmed executive branch appointees and all presidential appointments as well as working on congressional oversight investigations.

Kieran **WHITE** is seventeen years old and lives in Minnesota with his mom and dad. After helping to take care of his father who was diagnosed with ALS, Kieran made the decision to write about his experience in collaboration with poet and writer Wendy Angulo.

Emma **WOLFE**, the daughter of David Brattain, resides in Indianapolis, Indiana with her husband, Micah, and her five-month old daughter, Ella. She recently received her MSW at Indiana University-Purdue University Indianapolis and is presently working at Community Health Network as a Nicotine Dependence Therapist. In her spare time, she enjoys reading, writing, and spending time in nature.

Seeroon **YERETZIAN** is the author of four books, including the best-selling *Seeroon Darer: Armenian Ornate Initials*. Connect with her online at www.seeroonart.com.

ABOUT THE EDITOR

Eric **VALOR** displayed an adventurous curiosity from an early age, and a propensity for finding ways around difficult situations. He demonstrated this when at age twelve he taught himself to his family's IBM computer. Eric was an avid athlete—a black diamond skier and snowboarder, a surfer of those large waves at Scott Creek and Rio Nexpa, and a true waterman in every sense, having mastered sailing, swimming, and scuba diving. Having developed a refined culinary taste, Eric was a creative chef, sharing food and wine pairings and sophisticated recipes with friends and family. After his diagnosis with ALS, Eric began working with doctors and researchers in the search for a cure, and leveraged his expertise as an IT professional to connect with other PALS—Persons with ALS—though his website, blog, podcast and extensive social media activity.

"I refuse to go away. I am determined to continue to be of service regardless of my disability."

Manufactured by Amazon.ca
Bolton, ON

43726904R00092